DAY HIKES AROUND
BIG SUR

80 GREAT HIKES

by Robert Stone

Day Hike Books, Inc.
RED LODGE, MONTANA

Published by Day Hike Books, Inc.
P.O. Box 865
Red Lodge, Montana 59068

Distributed by The Globe Pequot Press
246 Goose Lane
P.O. Box 480
Guilford, CT 06437-0480
800-243-0495 (direct order) · 800-820-2329 (fax order)
www.globe-pequot.com

Photographs by Robert Stone
Design by Paula Doherty

The author has made every attempt to provide accurate information in this book. However, trail routes and features may change—please use common sense and forethought, and be mindful of your own capabilities. Let this book guide you, but be aware that each hiker assumes responsibility for their own safety. The author and publisher do not assume any responsibility for loss, damage or injury caused through the use of this book.

Cover photo: McWay Falls, Hike 43
Back cover photo: Garrapata State Park, Hike 12

Table of Contents

THE HIKES
Point Lobos State Reserve

Garrapata State Park

Rocky Point to Point Sur
Palo Colorado Road • Old Coast Road

Andrew Molera State Park

Pfeiffer Big Sur State Park

Julia Pfeiffer Burns State Park

Garland Ranch Regional Park

Interior Big Sur
Carmel Valley Road • Tassajara Road
Arroyo Seco Road

Limekiln State Park

Interior Big Sur
Nacimiento—Ferguson Road • Central Coast Ridge Road

Silver Peak Wilderness

South Big Sur Coast

Big Sur and its Trails

Big Sur is an awesome stretch of spectacular coastline where the Santa Lucia Mountains rise over 5,000 feet from the ocean. This magnificent landscape begins near Carmel at Point Lobos State Reserve and extends 75 miles south to Ragged Point in San Luis Obispo County, just south of the Monterey County line. The steep coastal mountain range and rugged shoreline isolate the Big Sur country, which maintains an unspoiled, rustic charm and relaxed, leisurely pace.

Perched on the western edge of the mountains, Highway 1 snakes along the rugged coast. The road hugs the edge of the precipitous cliffs and winds its way along the steep headlands. There are endless views of the scalloped coastline and the deep blue Pacific. Stunning bridges span numerous creeks and deep canyons. Other portions of the road cross flat, grassy marine terraces that gently slope to the eroded shoreline, with wave-worn rock pillars rising offshore.

There is much more to explore than the dramatic coastline, however. The Big Sur area also includes the Santa Lucia Range, running parallel to the coast in the heart of Big Sur country. The Ventana Wilderness, Silver Peak Wilderness and Los Padres National Forest lie within the mountain range. A network of hiking trails venture into the beautiful canyons and across the slopes and peaks, offering unparalleled views of the mountains merging with the coastline.

Day Hikes Around Big Sur includes a cross-section of 80 excellent hikes lying along the coastline and throughout the interior mountains. These hikes accommodate every level of hiking experience. The trails have been chosen for their scenery, variety and ability to be hiked within a day. Hikes range from easy beach strolls to strenuous mountain climbs with panoramic vistas. Highlights along the miles of trails include waterfalls, rivers, valleys, shady canyons, oak-studded meadows, huge stands of redwoods, tidepools, isolated beaches and stark vertical cliffs with crested ridges. You may enjoy these areas for a short time or the whole day. A quick glance at the hikes' summaries will allow you to choose a hike that is appropriate to your ability and desire.

Several state parks, two wilderness areas and five major watersheds lie within the Big Sur area. The diverse terrain is a hiker's paradise that has a well-designed trail system of more than 300 miles. An overall map of the 80 hikes is found on pages 10—11.

Point Lobos State Reserve (1,276 acres) is the crown jewel among California's state parks. The reserve has incredible bold headlands, ragged cliffs, sculpted coves, eroded inlets with tidepools, isolated beaches, craggy islets, marine terraces, large stands of Monterey cypress, rolling meadows and miles of hiking trails. Hikes 1—9 are found around Point Lobos.

Moving further down the coast are Garrapata State Park (2,879 acres), Andrew Molera State Park (4,800 acres), Pfeiffer Big Sur State Park (821 acres) and Julia Pfeiffer Burns State Park (3,500 acres). These coastal parks include a crenulated coastline of coves, hidden beaches, rocky points and pounding surf. Scenic meadows, canyons, rivers, waterfalls and peaks lie inland and upward along the ascending mountains. Several hikes lead to incredible vistas from the coastline to the interior wilderness. Hikes 10—13 and 22—45 are within these coastal state parks in central Big Sur.

Hikes 14—21 explore the region between Rocky Point and Point Sur. Highway 1 winds through the area across Bixby Bridge (spanning 714 feet at a height of 260 feet) and Rocky Creek Bridge (spanning 500 feet at a height of 150 feet). These are two of the most impressive canyon crossings along the highway. The Old Coast Road hike follows the original road before the Bixby Bridge was built.

Hikes 46—58 travel through the interior Santa Lucia Mountains and along the range's eastern side. There are several quiet strolls through old growth forests. Some creekside trails head up to high, rugged ridges. Other trails wind up canyons and gorges, with views back down to the valleys.

The southern Big Sur coastal area can be discovered in Hikes 59—80. The area is characterized by towering redwoods, forests, narrow canyons, waterfalls and cascades, marine terraces, steep ocean cliffs and expansive views. Limekiln State Park (Hikes 59—61) is home to redwoods, waterfalls and massive kilns from the 1880s. Several hikes are around Cone Peak (Hikes 62—67), which rises nearly a mile from the ocean in just over 3 miles. The Vicente Flat Trail, on the coastal side of Cone Peak, is one of the most scenic and diverse trails in Big Sur. The Silver Peak Wilderness offers access from the coast into the canyons and rivers flowing from the Santa Lucia Mountains. Furthest south (Hike 80) is Ragged Point, where a trail leads out to a peninsula overlooking the coast and mountain peaks.

The overall map on pages 10—11 identifies the general location of the hikes, state parks, wilderness areas and major access roads. Most hikes are accessed from Highway 1. A few inland roads, also shown on the overall map, access the higher reaches of the mountains from Highway 1. Each hike also includes its own map, a summary, driving and hiking directions and a overview of distance/time/elevation. In addition, many of the state parks have their own map in this book. To hike further, relevant maps are listed with each hike.

A few basic necessities will make your hike more enjoyable. Wear supportive, comfortable hiking shoes. Take along hats, sunscreen, sunglasses, drinking water, snacks and appropriate outerwear. Bring swimwear and outdoor gear if heading to the beaches. Ticks may be prolific and poison oak flourishes in the canyons and shady moist areas. Exercise caution by using insect repellent and staying on the trails.

From a leisurely walk to a vertical climb, you will experience Big Sur to its fullest by exploring on foot. Enjoy the trails!

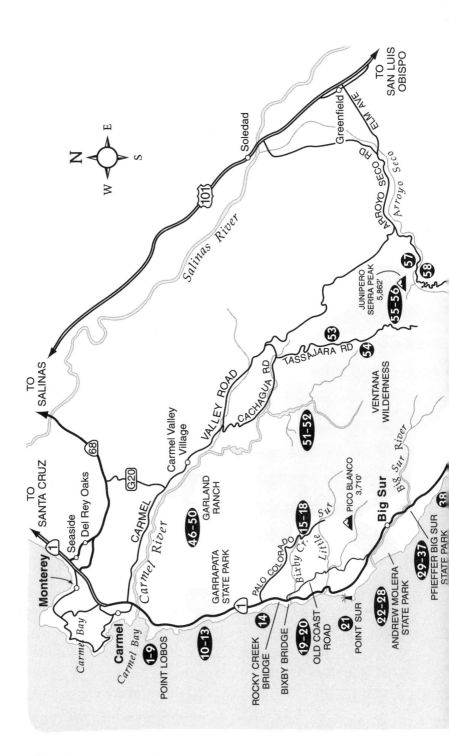

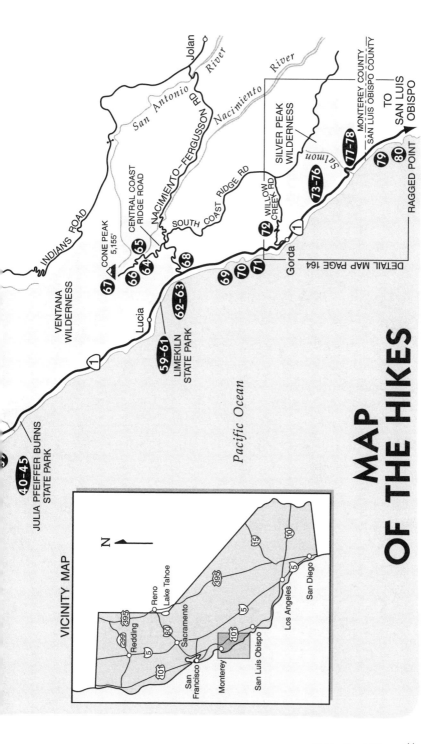

MAP
OF THE HIKES

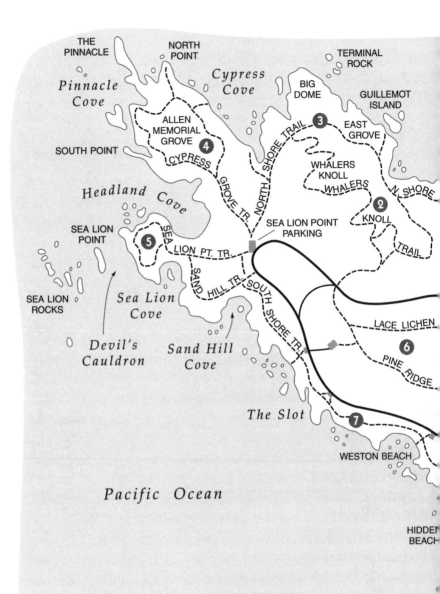

THE
PINNACLE

*Pinnacle
Cove*

NORTH
POINT

*Cypress
Cove*

TERMINAL
ROCK

BIG
DOME

GUILLEMOT
ISLAND

ALLEN
MEMORIAL
GROVE **4**

3

EAST
GROVE

SOUTH POINT

CYPRESS

WHALERS
KNOLL

Headland Cove

GROVE TR.

NORTH SHORE TRAIL

WHALERS

SEA

N. SHORE

2

KNOLL

SEA LION
POINT

5

SEA LION POINT
PARKING

TRAIL

LION PT. TR.

SAND HILL TR.

SOUTH SHORE TR.

LACE LICHEN

SEA LION
ROCKS

*Sea Lion
Cove*

6

PINE RIDGE

*Devil's
Cauldron*

*Sand Hill
Cove*

The Slot

7

WESTON BEACH

Pacific Ocean

HIDDEN
BEACH

POINT LOBOS
STATE RESERVE
HIKES 1–9

China

BIRD
ISLAND

Carmel Bay

Bluefish Cove

GRANITE POINT

Moss Cove

ICHXENTA POINT

CANNERY POINT

COAL CHUTE POINT

MOSS COVE TRAIL

1

TO CARMEL AND MONTEREY

TRAIL

Whalers Cove

GRANITE POINT TRAIL

WHALERS CABIN

GRANITE

WHALERS COVE ROAD

CARMELO MEADOW TRAIL

TRAIL

N

W — E

S

TRAIL

ENTRANCE STATION

MOUND MEADOW TR.

TRAIL

SOUTH PLATEAU TRAIL

1

9

BIRD ROCK PARKING

Cove

8

BIRD ISLAND TRAIL

GIBSON BEACH

PELICAN POINT

TO BIG SUR AND SAN LUIS OBISPO

WHALERS CABIN

Hike 1
Granite Point and Moss Cove Trails
Point Lobos State Reserve

Hiking distance: 2 miles round trip
Hiking time: 1 hour
Elevation gain: Near level
Maps: U.S.G.S. Monterey
Point Lobos State Reserve map

map
next page

Summary of hike: The Granite Point Trail begins from Whalers Cabin, a historic cabin built by fishermen in the 1850s that is currently a history museum. The trail curves around Whalers Cove to coastal overlooks on Coal Chute Point and Granite Point. Views extend across Carmel Bay and its sandy beaches to the golf courses at Pebble Beach. The hike continues on the Moss Cove Trail across open fields to Ichxenta Point, a low granite headland overlooking Monastery Beach.

Driving directions: From Highway 1 and Rio Road in Carmel, drive 2.2 miles south on Highway 1 to the signed Point Lobos State Reserve entrance. Turn right (west) to the entrance station. Continue 0.1 mile to the Whalers Cove turnoff. Turn right and drive 0.3 miles to the parking area at the end of the road. An entrance fee is required.

From the Big Sur Ranger Station, drive 24 miles north to the state park entrance and turn left.

Hiking directions: Walk back up the park road 0.1 mile to Whalers Cabin on the right. Across the road is the posted Granite Point Trail. Take the footpath left and follow the crescent-shaped Whalers Cove. Carmel and Pebble Beach are beautifully framed between Cannery Point and Coal Chute Point. Cross a bridge over a seasonal stream, passing a junction with the Carmelo Meadow Trail. At the east end of the cove, enter a forest of Monterey pines, curving left to an unsigned trail fork. Detour to the left and loop around Coal Chute Point through wind-sculpted Monterey pines and cypress. The trail overlooks Whalers Cove and The Pit, a small sandy beach in a sculpted cove with natural rock arches. Return to the Granite Point Trail, and head north above The Pit. Drop over a small knoll to views of Moss Cove, Escobar Rocks and Monastery Beach. Descend steps to the Moss Cove Trail at a 4-way junction. The sharp left fork leads down a draw to The Pit. The middle fork climbs steps to a loop around Granite Point. The right fork continues east on the Moss Cove Trail and crosses Hudson Meadow, a flat, grassy, marine terrace overlooking Moss Cove. Escobar Rocks forms a natural barrier to the beach cove. Carmelite Monastery can be seen peering out above the trees on the inland hillside. The trail ends at the northeast park boundary above Monastery Beach. Just before reaching the fenced boundary, a short path on the left ascends up to the rocky Ichxenta Point.

Hike 2
Whalers Knoll Trail
Point Lobos State Reserve

Hiking distance: 2 mile loop
Hiking time: 1 hour
Elevation gain: 180 feet
Maps: U.S.G.S. Monterey
   Point Lobos State Reserve map

**map
next page**

Summary of hike: Whalers Knoll was an historic lookout for spotting whales. The trail twists 200 feet up the hillside through an open Monterey pine forest draped with lace lichen. At the summit is a bench and panoramic views of Big Dome, Carmel Bay and the coastline to Pebble Beach. This hike begins from Whalers Cove and connects with Whalers Knoll via the North Shore Trail (Hike 3). The hike returns back down to Whalers Cabin, built by Chinese fisherman in the 1850s. The cabin now houses a museum.

Driving directions: Follow the driving directions for Hike 1.

Hiking directions: From the far north end of the parking area, take the signed North Shore Trail. Climb rock steps to an overlook of Cannery Point, Granite Point, Coal Chute Point, Whalers Cove, Carmel, Pebble Beach, Carmel Bay and the Santa Lucia Mountains. Stay left up a long flight of wooden steps to a trail split. The right fork leads to an overlook of Bluefish Cove. Bear left on the North Shore Trail towards Whalers Knoll. The serpentine path curves around Bluefish cove, passing the first junction with Whalers Knoll Trail, our return route. Begin the loop to the right, staying on the coastal path along the jagged cliffs. Pass a side trail on the right overlooking

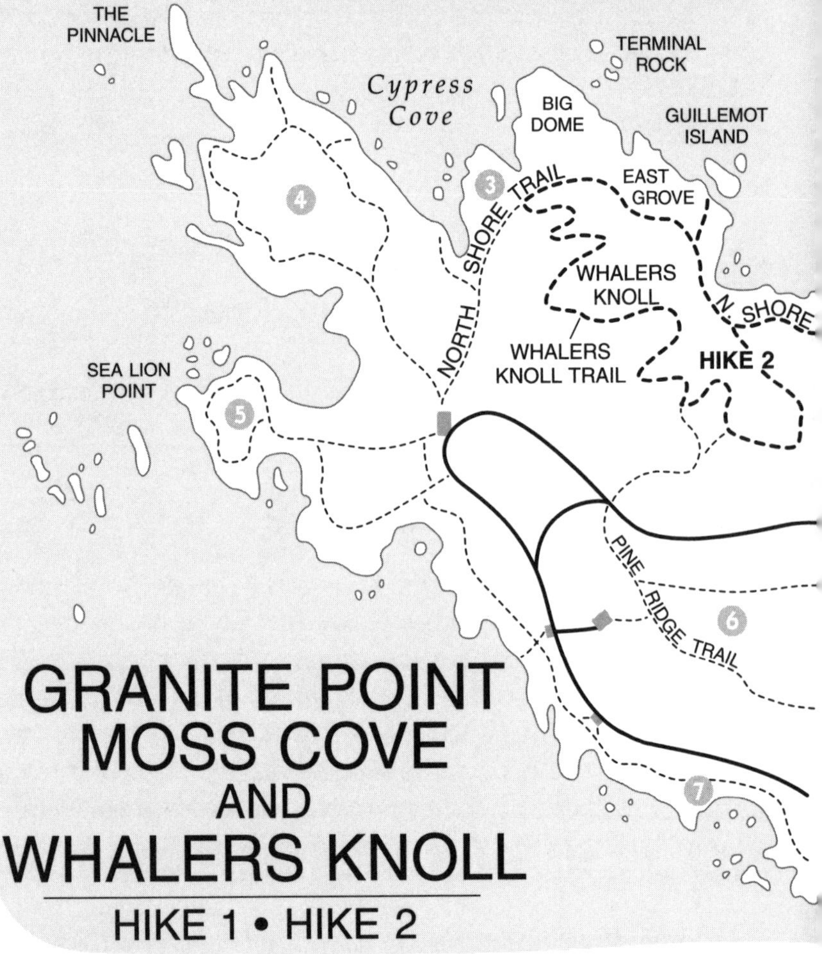

THE PINNACLE

TERMINAL ROCK

Cypress Cove

BIG DOME

GUILLEMOT ISLAND

NORTH SHORE TRAIL

EAST GROVE

WHALERS KNOLL

N. SHORE

SEA LION POINT

WHALERS KNOLL TRAIL

HIKE 2

PINE RIDGE TRAIL

GRANITE POINT
MOSS COVE
AND
WHALERS KNOLL
HIKE 1 • HIKE 2

Guillemot Island. Cross the inland side of Big Dome to the posted Whalers Knoll Trail on the left. Climb up the hillside, zigzagging through the Monterey pines to views of Sea Lion Point. Curve left, steadily climbing to the summit and a bench on the knoll. Savor the commanding views of Big Dome and Carmel Bay. Continue across the knoll and descend past two junctions with the Pine Ridge Trail on the right. Complete the loop back at Bluefish Cove on the North Shore Trail. Bear right to a signed junction on the right to the Whalers Cabin Trail, and descend through a native Monterey pine forest to the cabin at the park road. Take the park road 0.1 mile back to the left.

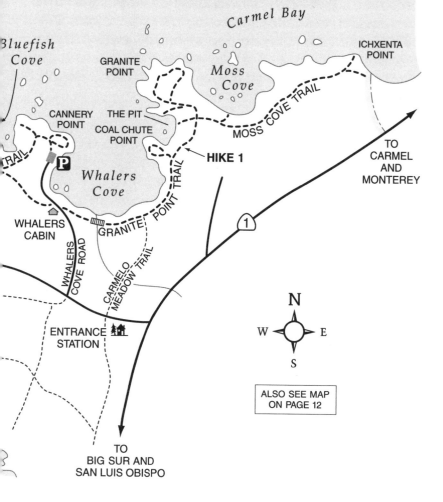

Hike 3
North Shore Trail
Point Lobos State Reserve

Hiking distance: 2.8 miles round trip
Hiking time: 1.5 hours
Elevation gain: 250 feet
Maps: U.S.G.S. Monterey
Point Lobos State Reserve map

Summary of hike: The North Shore Trail follows the exposed, rugged northern headlands past sheer granite cliffs and coves in Point Lobos State Reserve. A spur trail leads to an overlook of Guillemot Island, a rocky offshore nesting site for seabirds. A second spur trail leads to Cypress Cove and Old Veteran, a windswept, gnarled Monterey cypress clinging to the cliffs of the cove. The main trail winds through a canopy of Monterey pines and cypress draped with veils of lichen.

Driving directions: From Highway 1 and Rio Road in Carmel, drive 2.2 miles south on Highway 1 to the signed Point Lobos State Reserve entrance. Turn right (west) to the entrance station. Continue 0.1 mile to the Whalers Cove turnoff. Turn right and drive 0.3 miles to the parking area at the end of the road. An entrance fee is required.

From the Big Sur Ranger Station, drive 24 miles north to the state park entrance and turn left.

Hiking directions: Walk up the rock steps at the north end of the parking lot to a junction. The right fork loops around Cannery Point at the west end of Whalers Cove. Back at the first junction, ascend a long set of steps, and enter the forest to another junction. The short right fork leads to an overlook of Bluefish Cove. On the North Shore Trail, curve around the cove to a junction with the Whalers Knoll Trail on the left (Hike 2). Continue weaving along the coastal cliffs around Bluefish Cove to a short spur trail leading to the Guillemot Island overlook. Back on the main trail, continue northwest past a native grove of Monterey cypress in East Grove. Cross a saddle past Big Dome to a second junction with the Whalers Knoll Trail. At Cypress Cove, detour on the Old Veteran Trail to view the twisted Monterey cypress and the cove. The North Shore Trail ends in the coastal scrub at the trailhead to the Cypress Grove Trail (Hike 4) by the Sea Lion Point parking area. Return along the same trail.

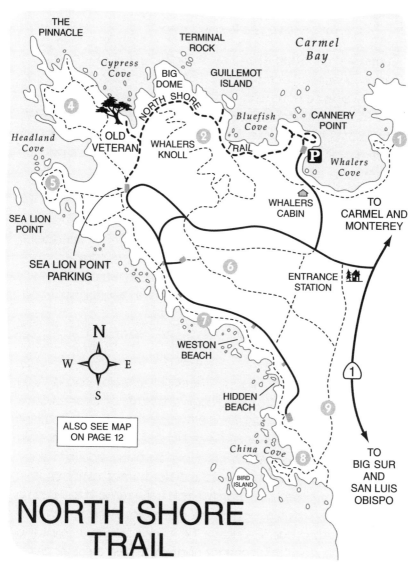

NORTH SHORE TRAIL

Hike 4
Cypress Grove Trail
Point Lobos State Reserve

Hiking distance: 0.8 miles round trip
Hiking time: 30 minutes
Elevation gain: 100 feet
Maps: U.S.G.S. Monterey
        Point Lobos State Reserve map

Summary of hike: The Cypress Grove Trail is a clifftop loop trail around Allan Memorial Grove. The trail passes through one of only two natural stands of Monterey cypress in the world. The hike loops around the cliffs overlooking Cypress Cove, Pinnacle Cove, South Point, Headland Cove and The Pinnacle, a narrow peninsula at the northernmost point in the reserve.

Driving directions: From Highway 1 and Rio Road in Carmel, drive 2.2 miles south on Highway 1 to the signed Point Lobos State Reserve entrance. Turn right (west) to the entrance station. Continue 0.7 miles to the Sea Lion Point parking area on the right side of the road. An entrance fee is required.

From the Big Sur Ranger Station, drive 24 miles north to the state park entrance and turn left.

Hiking directions: Two well-marked trails begin on the north end of the parking lot. To the right is the North Shore Trail (Hike 3). Take the Cypress Grove Trail to the left through coastal scrub 0.2 miles to a trail split. Begin the loop around Allan Memorial Grove to the right. Follow the edge of Cypress Cove to a short spur trail on the right, leading to an overlook of Cypress Cove and views of Carmel Bay. Back on the loop, pass through an indigenous Monterey cypress grove. A spur trail at the north end of the loop leads to the North Point overlook with views of The Pinnacle. Back on the main trail, granite steps lead up to Pinnacle Cove on a rocky promontory with stunning views of South Point and Headland Cove. Continue past South Point and Headland Cove, completing the loop. Return to the trailhead.

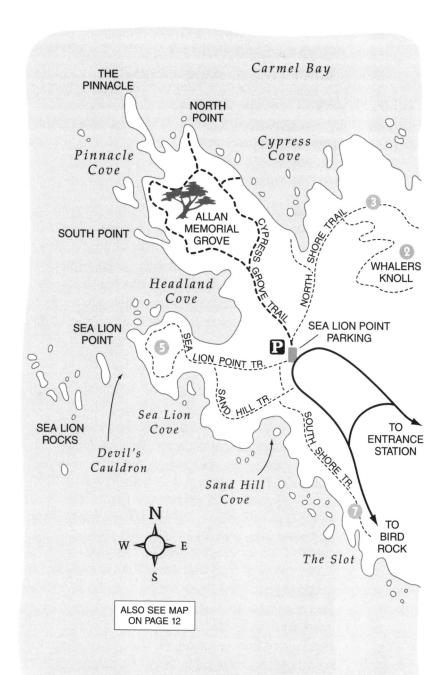

CYPRESS GROVE TRAIL

Hike 5
Sea Lion Point Trail
Point Lobos State Reserve

Hiking distance: 0.7 miles round trip
Hiking time: 30 minutes
Elevation gain: 50 feet
Maps: U.S.G.S. Monterey
Point Lobos State Reserve map

Summary of hike: The Sea Lion Point Trail leads to a spectacular, surreal landscape on the coastal bluff above Headland Cove. From the bluffs are vistas of Sea Lion Cove, Sea Lion Rocks and the churning whitewater at Devil's Cauldron. The offshore sea stacks and rocky coves are abundant with sea otters, harbor seals and barking California sea lions. The return route follows the eroded cliffs between Sea Lion Cove and Sand Hill Cove.

Driving directions: From Highway 1 and Rio Road in Carmel, drive 2.2 miles south on Highway 1 to the signed Point Lobos State Reserve entrance. Turn right (west) to the entrance station. Continue 0.7 miles to the Sea Lion Point parking area on the right side of the road. An entrance fee is required.

From the Big Sur Ranger Station, drive 24 miles north to the state park entrance and turn left.

Hiking directions: From the far west end of the parking area, take the signed Sea Lion Point Trail. The path crosses through coastal scrub to a trail split. Stay to the right, heading toward the point. At the crest of the rocky bluffs is a trail junction and an incredible vista point. The views include South Point, The Pinnacle, Sea Lion Cove, Devil's Cauldron and Sea Lion Rocks. On the right, descend the natural staircase of weathered rock to the headland. From the lower level, circle the point around Headland Cove to close up views of Devil's Cauldron and Sea Lion Rocks. Loop back around by the sandy beach at Sea Lion Cove. Return up the steps to the overlook. Proceed south on

Sand Hill Trail, following the cliffs above Sea Lion Cove and Sand Hill Cove. Pass the South Shore Trail on the right (Hike 7), and complete the loop back at the parking area.

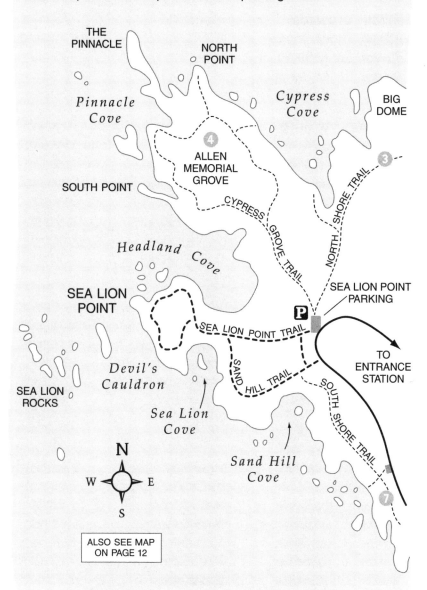

SEA LION POINT

Hike 6
Lace Lichen—Mound Meadow—Pine Ridge Loop
Point Lobos State Reserve

Hiking distance: 1.2 mile loop
Hiking time: 30 minutes
Elevation gain: Level
Maps: U.S.G.S. Monterey
　　　　Point Lobos State Reserve map

Summary of hike: Lace lichen is a combination of fungus and algae that looks like a stringy beard hanging from the tree branches. The Lace Lichen Trail parallels the park road through a cool and humid pine and oak forest draped with lace lichen. Pine Ridge Trail crosses through open forests of native Monterey pine and coastal live oak with views of Bird Island and the ocean. The Mound Meadow Trail crosses an ancient marine terrace on the border of a pine forest and a meadow, a foraging ground for deer. These three trails are combined to form a loop.

Driving directions: From Highway 1 and Rio Road in Carmel, drive 2.2 miles south on Highway 1 to the signed Point Lobos State Reserve entrance. Turn right (west) to the entrance station. Continue 1 mile to the Piney Woods turnoff on the left. Turn left and drive 0.1 mile to the Piney Woods Picnic Area at the end of the road. An entrance fee is required.

From the Big Sur Ranger Station, drive 24 miles north to the state park entrance and turn left.

Hiking directions: Take the signed Pine Ridge Trail east through a shaded forest canopy to a T-junction. Begin the loop to the left through a predominantly Monterey pine forest. At the posted junction, leave the Pine Ridge Trail, and bear right on the Lace Lichen Trail. The level path weaves through the forest of Monterey pine and coastal live oak that is heavily draped in lace lichen. Continue to a signed trail fork near the park entrance road by Whalers Cove Road. Bear right on Mound Meadow Trail, and meander through the open forest to a posted 4-way junction with the Pine Ridge Trail. The Mound Meadow Trail continues south to the coastline near Hidden Beach. Take the Pine Ridge Trail to the right, and follow the ridge through the forest to a bench at a vista point. The views extend south to Mound Meadow, Weston Beach, Bird Island, Pelican Point and Yankee Point by the Carmel Highlands. Complete the loop a short distance ahead.

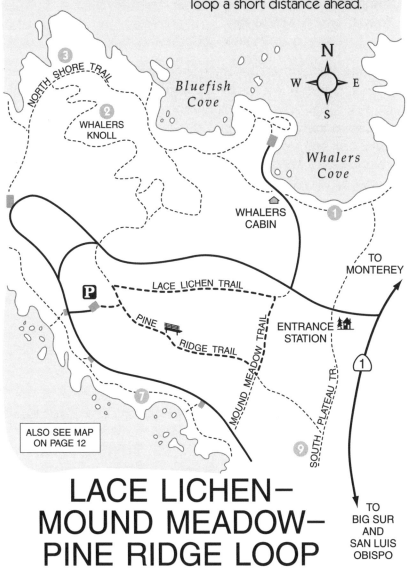

LACE LICHEN–
MOUND MEADOW–
PINE RIDGE LOOP

Hike 7
South Shore Trail
Point Lobos State Reserve

Hiking distance: 2 miles round trip
Hiking time: 1 hour
Elevation gain: 30 feet
Maps: U.S.G.S. Monterey
Point Lobos State Reserve map

Summary of hike: The South Shore Trail explores the eroded sandstone terrain along the jagged southern ridges and troughs of the reserve. The trail begins near Bird Island and ends by Sea Lion Point, weaving past tidepools and rocky beach coves tucked between the cliffs. The beach coves include rock-encased Hidden Beach and Weston Beach, with multi-colored pebbles and flat rock slabs. The trail continues past The Slot, a narrow channel bound by rock, and the 100-foot cliffs at Sand Hill Cove.

Driving directions: From Highway 1 and Rio Road in Carmel, drive 2.2 miles south on Highway 1 to the signed Point Lobos State Reserve entrance. Turn right (west) to the entrance kiosk. Continue 1.6 miles to the Bird Rock parking area at the end of the road. An entrance fee is required.

From the Big Sur Ranger Station, drive 24 miles north to the state park entrance and turn left.

Hiking directions: The signed South Shore Trail begins at the north end of the parking area overlooking China Cove. Head north (right), walking along the edge of the cliffs to a junction with the Hidden Beach path on the left. Stone steps descend to the oval beach cove. Return to the main trail and follow the contours of the jagged coastline past numerous coves, tidepools and rock islands. A few connector trails on the right lead to parking areas along the park road. At Sand Hill Cove, steps lead up to a T-junction with the Sand Hill Trail. This is our turnaround spot. Return along the same trail.

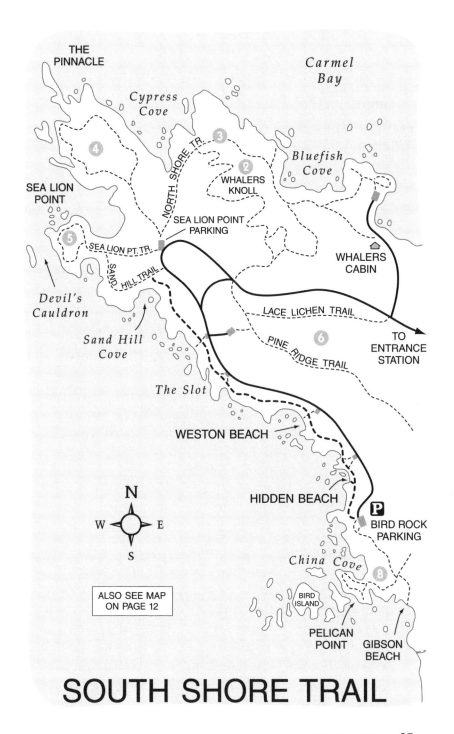

THE PINNACLE

Carmel Bay

Cypress Cove

SEA LION POINT

Bluefish Cove

WHALERS KNOLL

NORTH SHORE TR.

SEA LION POINT PARKING

SEA LION PT. TR.

WHALERS CABIN

Devil's Cauldron

SAND HILL TRAIL

LACE LICHEN TRAIL

Sand Hill Cove

PINE RIDGE TRAIL

TO ENTRANCE STATION

The Slot

WESTON BEACH

HIDDEN BEACH

N
W E
S

🅿 BIRD ROCK PARKING

ALSO SEE MAP ON PAGE 12

China Cove

BIRD ISLAND

PELICAN POINT

GIBSON BEACH

SOUTH SHORE TRAIL

Hike 8
Bird Island Trail
China Cove—Pelican Point—Gibson Beach
Point Lobos State Reserve

Hiking distance: 0.8 miles round trip
Hiking time: 30 minutes
Elevation gain: 20 feet
Maps: U.S.G.S. Monterey
      Point Lobos State Reserve map

Summary of hike: The Bird Island Trail follows the rocky coastline between a Monterey pine forest and the cliffs overlooking the sea (cover photo). The trail passes chasms, arches, sea caves and the white sand beaches of China Cove and Gibson Beach. Both beach coves are surrounded by granite cliffs with staircase access. The hike loops around Pelican Point with close views of Bird Island, inhabited by nesting colonies of cormorants and brown pelicans.

Driving directions: From Highway 1 and Rio Road in Carmel, drive 2.2 miles south on Highway 1 to the signed Point Lobos State Reserve entrance. Turn right (west) to the entrance kiosk. Continue 1.6 miles to the Bird Rock parking area at the end of the road. An entrance fee is required.

From the Big Sur Ranger Station, drive 24 miles north to the state park entrance and turn left.

Hiking directions: Ascend the steps at the south end of the parking lot, and head through a Monterey pine forest to an overlook of China Cove and Bird Island. Follow the cliffside path as it curves around the head of China Cove to a signed junction. A long set of stairs to the right descends the cliffs to the sandy beach and cave in China Cove. After exploring the beach, return to the Bird Island Trail. Continue along the cliffs to a posted T-junction and overlook of the crescent-shaped Gibson Beach below the Carmel Highlands. For a short detour to Gibson Beach, bear left on the South Plateau Trail a few yards to the posted beach access on the right. Descend a long flight of steps to the sandy beach at the base of the cliffs. Returning to the T-junction, head west towards Pelican Point through coastal scrub to a trail split. The paths loop around the flat bench, overlooking Bird Island, the magnificent offshore rock outcroppings, chasms, sea caves and China Cove. Complete the loop and return along the same path.

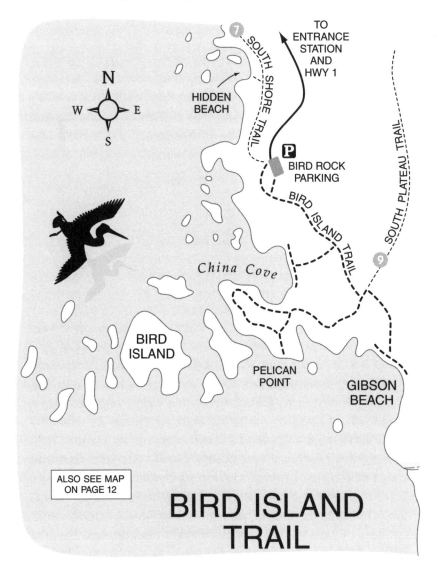

BIRD ISLAND
TRAIL

Hike 9
South Plateau—Mound Meadow Loop
Point Lobos State Reserve

Hiking distance: 1.6 mile loop
Hiking time: 1 hour
Elevation gain: 100 feet
Maps: U.S.G.S. Monterey
       Point Lobos State Reserve map

Summary of hike: The South Plateau Trail connects the white sands of China Cove and Gibson Beach with the entrance station. The nature trail crosses Vierra's Knoll as it winds through a forest of Monterey pine and coastal live oak. Along the trail are 12 interpretive stations about the plants and animals. (An interpretive pamphlet is available at the entrance station.) The hike returns on the Mound Meadow Trail across an ancient marine terrace. The hike offers access to China Cove, Gibson Beach and Hidden Beach, a pocket beach surrounded by rocks.

Driving directions: Same as Hike 8.

Hiking directions: Take the posted Bird Island Trail at the south (far) end of the parking lot. Climb a long set of steps and curve along the cliffs overlooking China Cove and Bird Island. A stair access leads to the gorgeous pocket beach. Loop around China Cove towards Gibson Beach and a T-junction. The Bird Island Trail (Hike 8) goes right. Take the left fork on the South Plateau Trail a short distance to the Gibson Beach access on the right. For a detour to Gibson Beach, bear right and descend a long flight of steps to the sandy crescent beach. Returning to the South Plateau Trail, wind through chaparral to Vierra's Knoll, and enter a Monterey pine forest. Gently descend from the knoll into a forest of twisted live oaks draped with lace lichen. Wind through the dense forest, passing the Pine Ridge Trail on the left. Continue straight, parallel to Highway 1, through large patches of poison oak, wood mint and blackberries. The trail ends by the park entrance. Follow the park entrance road 0.1

mile to the paved service road on the left across from Whalers Cove Road. Walk ten yards to the left, and pick up the signed trail at a Y-junction on the right. The Lace Lichen Trail (Hike 6) forks right. Take the Mound Meadow Trail to the left, and meander through the pine forest, passing a 4-way junction with the Pine Ridge Trail. Continue south towards the ocean, which can be seen through the trees. Emerge from the forest at the park road. Cross the road to the South Shore Trail at a small rocky beach cove. Bear left and follow the coastline 0.2 miles — passing numerous ocean inlets and the Hidden Beach access — back to the parking lot.

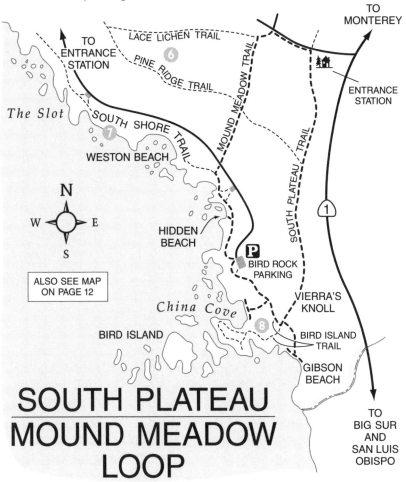

SOUTH PLATEAU
MOUND MEADOW
LOOP

Hike 10
Soberanes Canyon Trail
Garrapata State Park

Hiking distance: 3 miles round trip
Hiking time: 1.5 hours
Elevation gain: 900 feet
Maps: U.S.G.S. Soberanes Point
        Garrapata State Park map

Summary of hike: The Soberanes Canyon Trail follows Soberanes Creek up the wet, narrow canyon through magnificent stands of huge redwoods in Garrapata State Park. The trail crosses Soberanes Creek seven times before climbing up to the head of the canyon. At the top, the trail emerges onto the dry, chaparral covered hillside with panoramic views.

Driving directions: From Highway 1 and Rio Road in Carmel, drive 6.8 miles south on Highway 1 to the unsigned parking turnouts on either side of the road. The turnouts are located by a tin roof barn on the inland side of the highway.

From the Big Sur Ranger Station, drive 19.4 miles north to the parking turnouts.

Hiking directions: From the inland side of the highway, walk past the trailhead gate, following the old ranch road through a cypress grove. Curve left around the barn and down to Soberanes Creek. Cross the bridge to a signed junction. The left fork leads to Rocky Ridge (Hike 11), the rounded 1,435-foot peak. Take the right fork and head up the canyon along the north side of the creek. Cross another footbridge and curve left, staying in Soberanes Canyon. Recross the creek on a third footbridge and head steadily uphill. Rock hop over the creek, entering a beautiful redwood forest. Follow the watercourse through the redwoods to a lush grotto. The trail crosses the creek three consecutive times, then climbs a long series of steps. Traverse the canyon wall on a cliff ledge, climbing high above the creek. Switchbacks descend back to the creek.

Climb up more steps to the head of the canyon. The lush canyon gives way to the dry sage covered hills and an unsigned trail split. This is our turnaround spot.

For a longer hike, take the left fork up the steep exposed slopes towards Rocky Ridge—Hike 11.

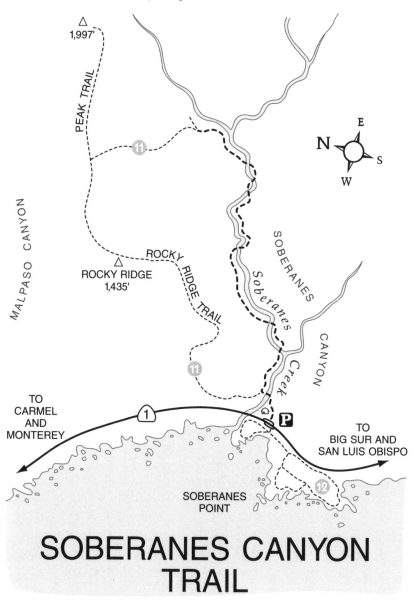

SOBERANES CANYON TRAIL

Hike 11
Rocky Ridge—Soberanes Canyon Loop
Garrapata State Park

Hiking distance: 6 mile loop
Hiking time: 3 hours
Elevation gain: 1,600 feet
Maps: U.S.G.S. Soberanes Point
     Garrapata State Park map

Summary of hike: Rocky Ridge is a 1,435-foot rounded grassy peak between Soberanes Canyon and Malpaso Canyon in Garrapata State Park. The steep trail up to Rocky Ridge follows a dry, exposed hillside. The payoff is sweeping views of the ocean, coastline and mountain. This hike is strenuous and only recommended for serious hikers.

Driving directions: Same as Hike 10.

Hiking directions: From the inland side of the highway, walk past the trailhead gate, following the old ranch road through a cypress grove. Curve left around the barn, and descend to Soberanes Creek. The rounded mountain peak straight ahead is Rocky Ridge. Cross the bridge to a signed junction. The right fork heads up Soberanes Canyon (Hike 10), our return route. Bear left (north) parallel to the highway on the lower grassy slopes of Rocky Ridge. Cross a couple of gullies to a trail split. The left fork returns to the highway. Take the right fork, which curves right and ascends the rugged, sage covered slope to a ridge. Begin a much steeper ascent, reaching a knoll. After resting, cross a saddle, finally reaching Rocky Ridge at 1,435 feet. Continue uphill, around the ridge overlooking the Malpaso Creek drainage, to a junction with the Peak Trail (North Ridge Trail). The 0.7 mile spur trail bears left, gaining 300 feet to the highest point in the state park at 1,977 feet. Continue the loop on the right fork towards Soberanes Canyon. Descend down the south-facing ridge on the very steep and rocky trail, losing 1,000 feet in less than a mile. At the head of Soberanes Canyon, follow the north canyon wall down to Soberanes Creek on the shady canyon floor. The lush path follows the watercourse through a redwood forest with six creek crossings—Hike 10.

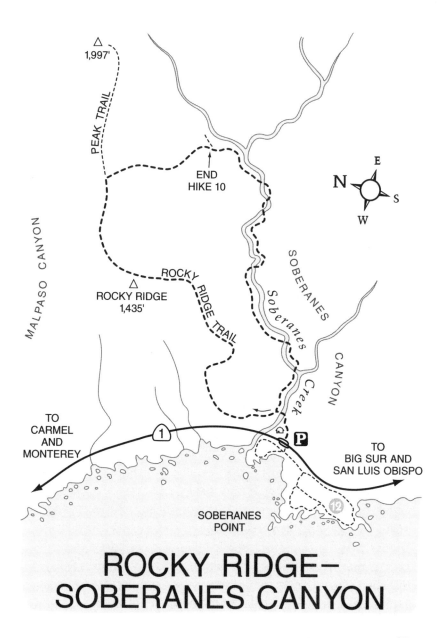

ROCKY RIDGE– SOBERANES CANYON

Hike 12
Soberanes Point Trails
Garrapata State Park

Hiking distance: 1.8 miles round trip
Hiking time: 1 hour
Elevation gain: 200 feet
Maps: U.S.G.S. Soberanes Point
        Garrapata State Park map

Summary of hike: The undeveloped Garrapata State Park stretches along four miles of scenic coastline and extends into the inland mountains. These coastal bluff trails along Soberanes Point lead to a myriad of crenelated coves, hidden beaches and rocky points (back cover photo). Soberanes Point, a popular whale-watching spot, is a serrated headland backed by Whale Peak, a 280-foot hill overlooking the Pacific. The trail circles the headland, then climbs Whale Peak. From the summit are 360-degree panoramic views from Yankee Point in the north to Point Sur in the south.

Driving directions: From Highway 1 and Rio Road in Carmel, drive 6.8 miles south on Highway 1 to the unsigned parking turnouts on both sides of the road. The turnouts are located by a tin roof barn on the inland side of the highway.

    From the Big Sur Ranger Station, drive 19.4 miles north to the parking turnouts.

Hiking directions: Walk through the trailhead gate on the ocean side of the highway, bearing left through a grove of cypress trees. Continue south towards Soberanes Point and Whale Peak, curving around the north side of the peak to an unsigned junction. The left fork circles the base of the hill. Take the right fork west along the coastal terrace to the northwest end of Soberanes Point. Follow the ocean cliffs to the southern point. From the south end, the trail returns toward Highway 1 by a gate. Stay on the footpath to the left, following the hillside trail to an unsigned junction. The left fork climbs a quarter mile up to the grassy ridge of Whale Peak. A trail follows the crest to the two summits. Return to the base of the hill, and continue to the north to complete the loop. Go to the right, back to the trailhead.

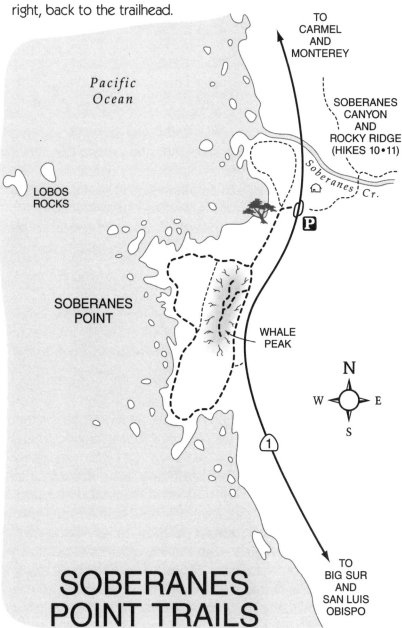

TO
CARMEL
AND
MONTEREY

Pacific
Ocean

SOBERANES
CANYON
AND
ROCKY RIDGE
(HIKES 10•11)

Soberanes Cr.

LOBOS
ROCKS

P

SOBERANES
POINT

WHALE
PEAK

N
W E
S

1

TO
BIG SUR
AND
SAN LUIS
OBISPO

SOBERANES
POINT TRAILS

Hike 13
Garrapata Beach and Bluff Trail
Garrapata State Park

Hiking distance: 1–2.5 miles round trip
Hiking time: 1 hour
Elevation gain: 50 feet
Maps: U.S.G.S. Soberanes Point
      Garrapata State Park map

Summary of hike: Garrapata Beach sits near the southern border of this 2,879-acre state park. The pristine beach is a half-mile crescent of white sand with rocky tidepools. At the south end, Garrapata Creek empties into the Pacific through a granite gorge. This trail follows the bluffs through an ice plant meadow above the beach. Stairways access the beach. This beautiful sandy strand is an unofficial clothing-optional beach.

Driving directions: From Highway 1 and Rio Road in Carmel, drive 9.6 miles south on Highway 1 to the unsigned parking turnouts on both sides of the highway. The turnouts are located between two historic bridges—1.2 miles south of the Granite Creek Bridge and 0.2 miles north of the Garrapata Creek Bridge.

From the Big Sur Ranger Station, drive 16.6 miles north to the parking turnouts.

Hiking directions: Walk through gate 19 and descend a few steps. Follow the path to the edge of the oceanfront cliffs and a trail split. To the left, steps lead down the cliffs to the sandy beach. From the beach, head south (left) a short distance to Garrapata Creek and the jagged rocks at the point. To the right, beachcomb for a half mile along the base of the cliffs to the north point. Back at the blufftop junction, the bluff trail heads north, following the cliff's edge into a ravine. Steps lead down to Doud Creek and a trail split. The left path leads to Garrapata Beach. To the right, the trail crosses the drainage. Steps lead back up the bluffs to a junction. Take the left fork to continue along the bluffs. Choose your own turnaround spot.

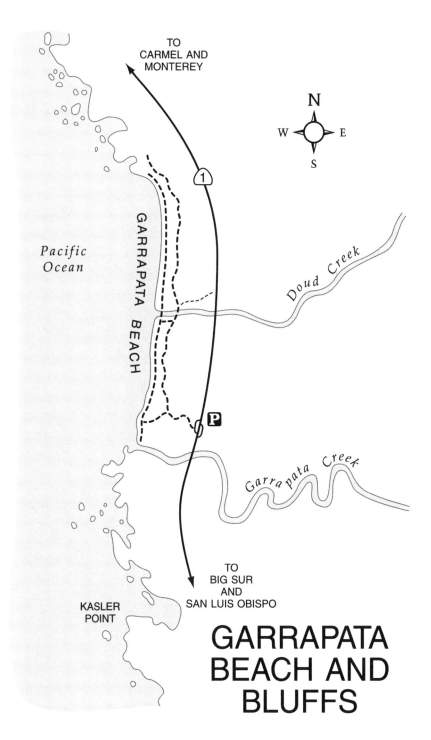

TO
CARMEL AND
MONTEREY

N
W   E
S

1

Pacific
Ocean

GARRAPATA BEACH

Doud Creek

P

Garrapata Creek

TO
BIG SUR
AND
SAN LUIS OBISPO

KASLER
POINT

GARRAPATA BEACH AND BLUFFS

Hike 14
Rocky Point

Hiking distance: 1.3 miles round trip
Hiking time: 30 minutes
Elevation gain: 100 feet
Maps: U.S.G.S. Soberanes Point

Summary of hike: Rocky Point is a dramatic rock formation jutting out to sea with powerful waves crashing against the rocks. The point has a series of summits and overlooks with awesome coastal views that include Rocky Creek Bridge, spanning 500 feet and hovering 150 feet above the creek; the Point Sur Lightstation, jutting out to sea; and the scalloped coastline and offshore rocks. This area can be hazardous due to unexpected large waves and jagged rocky ledges. Step carefully and use extreme caution. Parking is available at the trailhead for patrons of the Rocky Point Restaurant, cutting 0.8 miles off the round trip mileage.

Driving directions: From Highway 1 and Rio Road in Carmel, drive 10.7 miles south on Highway 1 to the signed Rocky Point Restaurant entrance. Park in the large turnout on the right side of the highway, 0.2 miles south of the entrance. There is also a small turnout on the left (inland) side of the highway directly across from the entrance.

From the Big Sur Ranger Station, drive 16 miles north to Rocky Point, located 0.4 miles north of Palo Colorado Road.

Hiking directions: Follow Highway 1 northbound 0.2 miles to Rocky Point Road. Follow the road west towards the ocean and the Rocky Point Restaurant. Curve left to the south end of the parking lot by the "Hazardous Waves" sign and footpath at 0.4 miles. Walk towards the point and the first summit. Views open up to the numerous rock formations and crevices, with vistas of Rocky Creek Bridge and the jagged coastline to the south. Skirt around the right side of the summit to a trail split. Detour on the left fork to a point overlooking rock caves and crashing whitewater. Return to the junction and descend on the right fork down a grassy saddle to an overlook of the jagged rock fingers, water inlets and a natural arch. Ascend to the west, climbing out of the saddle to the perch on the summit of Rocky Point.

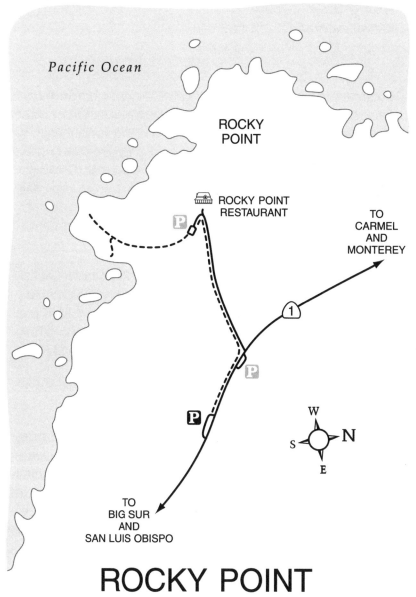

ROCKY POINT

Hike 15
Skinner Ridge Trail to
Skinner Ridge Overlook

Hiking distance: 4.2 miles round trip
Hiking time: 2.5 hours
Elevation gain: 1,400 feet
Maps: U.S.G.S. Big Sur and Mt. Carmel
      Ventana Wilderness Map

Summary of hike: Skinner Ridge Trail begins from Bottchers Gap at over 2,000 feet. The trail follows the upper reaches of Mill Creek through the shade of oaks and madrones, reaching the crest of Skinner Ridge at the Ventana Wilderness boundary. From the 3,400-foot ridge are spectacular vistas southwest of the Little Sur watershed, Pico Blanco's white marble cone, the folded layers and ridges of the coast range and the Pacific Ocean. The trail continues to Devil's Peak and Mount Carmel (Hike 16).

Driving directions: From Highway 1 and Rio Road in Carmel, drive 11.1 miles south on Highway 1 to the signed Palo Colorado Road, located 0.4 miles south of Rocky Point. Turn inland and drive 7.6 miles up the winding mountain road to the Bottchers Gap parking lot at the end of the paved road. A parking fee is required.

From the Big Sur Ranger Station, drive 15.1 miles north to Palo Colorado Road.

Hiking directions: From the upper end of the parking lot, take the posted Skinner Ridge Trail into the forest, skirting the campground sites on the left. Pass through oak groves and chaparral. The northwest views extend into the Mill Creek drainage and across several ridges to the ocean. For a short distance, the trail parallels Mill Creek, then drops down to the creek. Ascend the hillside and wind through the woods, crossing a stream in a fern-lined gully. Cross two additional tributary streams, reaching Skinner Ridge on a sloping meadow at 2.2

miles. Curve left and head north up the grassy meadow to a knoll and a magnificent overlook. After savoring the views, return along the same trail. To hike to Mount Carmel, continue with the next hike.

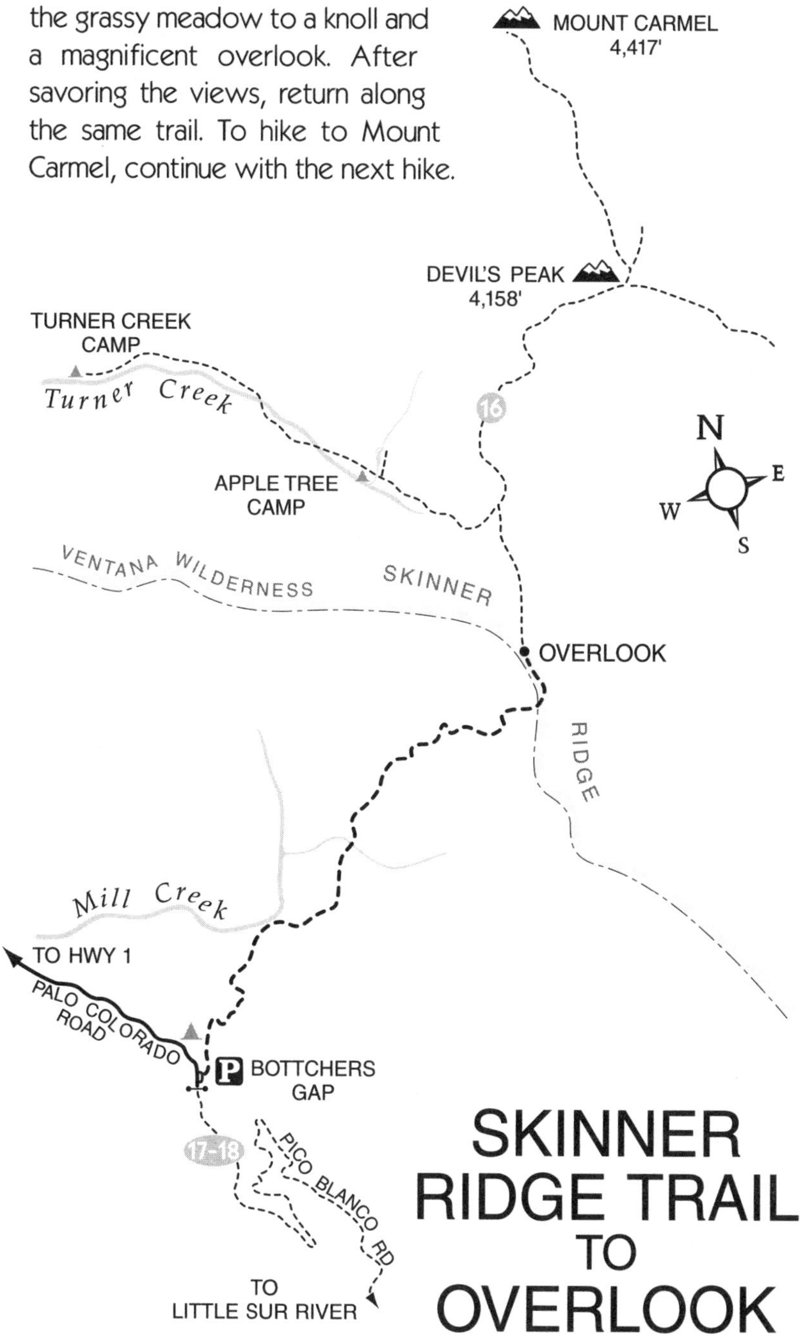

MOUNT CARMEL
4,417'

DEVIL'S PEAK
4,158'

TURNER CREEK
CAMP

Turner Creek

APPLE TREE
CAMP

VENTANA WILDERNESS

SKINNER

16

N
E
W
S

OVERLOOK

RIDGE

Mill Creek

TO HWY 1

PALO COLORADO ROAD

P BOTTCHERS
GAP

17-18

PICO BLANCO RD

TO
LITTLE SUR RIVER

SKINNER RIDGE TRAIL TO OVERLOOK

Hike 16
Skinner Ridge Trail to Mount Carmel

Hiking distance: 9.6 miles round trip
Hiking time: 5 hours
Elevation gain: 2,500 feet
Maps: U.S.G.S. Big Sur and Mt. Carmel
    Ventana Wilderness Map

Summary of hike: Mount Carmel (4,417 feet) is the highest peak in the northwest portion of the Ventana Wilderness. From the summit are endless vistas across the rugged mountainous interior to the Pacific Ocean, including prominent Pico Blanco, Ventana Double Cone, the Little Sur watershed and Monterey Bay. The trail follows Skinner Ridge and skirts the twin summits of Devil's Peak en route to Mount Carmel.

Driving directions: Same as Hike 15.

Hiking directions: Follow the hiking directions of the Skinner Ridge Trail—Hike 15—to the overlook on Skinner Ridge. Walk along the ridge past oaks and madrones for 0.2 miles. Leave the ridge and descend along the path to a saddle and posted junction with the Turner Creek Trail on the left. Continue straight ahead and ascend the hillside through thick brush and spectacular vistas. Over the next mile, steadily climb up the steeper grade, passing through oak, manzanita and madrone groves, to a sandy ridge near Devil's Peak. Follow the ridge to the left, viewing Mount Carmel to the north and Pico Blanco to the south. Curve around the right side of the second summit of Devil's Peak to a trail split. The right fork (straight ahead) leads to Comings Camp and Big Pines. Curve left 30 yards to a second fork. Curve to the left again, and descend to a grassy saddle. Cross the saddle and follow the ridge through oak groves and dense oak scrub that crowd the trail. The path ends at the summit of Mount Carmel, crowned by a 10-foot granite rock outcropping and an old climbing pole. A survey pin in the rock marks the summit. Climb the rock for a 360-degree panorama.

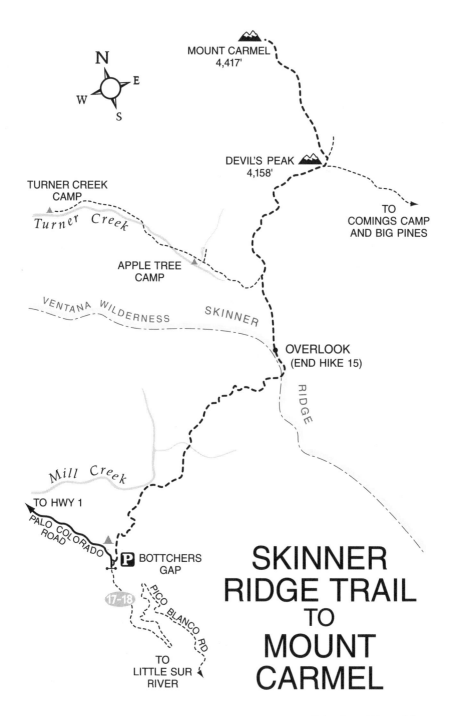

MOUNT CARMEL
4,417'

DEVIL'S PEAK
4,158'

TO
COMINGS CAMP
AND BIG PINES

TURNER CREEK
CAMP

Turner Creek

APPLE TREE
CAMP

VENTANA WILDERNESS

SKINNER

OVERLOOK
(END HIKE 15)

RIDGE

Mill Creek

TO HWY 1

PALO COLORADO ROAD

BOTTCHERS
GAP

17-18

PICO BLANCO RD.

TO
LITTLE SUR
RIVER

SKINNER RIDGE TRAIL TO MOUNT CARMEL

Hike 17
Little Sur River Camp

Hiking distance: 5.6 miles round trip
Hiking time: 3 hours
Elevation gain: 1,200 feet
Maps: U.S.G.S. Big Sur
  Ventana Wilderness Map

Summary of hike: Little Sur River Camp sits on a scenic riverside flat amidst tanbark oak trees and towering redwoods. The hike begins on a mountain saddle at Bottchers Gap. The vehicle-restricted road winds down the canyon into the Little Sur watershed with magnificent views of Pico Blanco's north face. A series of campsites with fire pits and benches stretch along the cascading river.

Driving directions: From Highway 1 and Rio Road in Carmel, drive 11.1 miles south on Highway 1 to the signed Palo Colorado Road, located 0.4 miles south of Rocky Point. Turn inland and drive 7.6 miles up the winding mountain road to the Bottchers Gap parking lot at the end of the paved road. A parking fee is required.

From the Big Sur Ranger Station, drive 15.1 miles north on Highway 1 to Palo Colorado Road.

Hiking directions: Take the posted Pico Blanco Road at the lower end of the parking lot. Walk around the locked vehicle gate, and descend on the unpaved road. At the first left horseshoe bend is a great close-up view of Pico Blanco and Dani Ridge, which extends to the Pacific Ocean. Continue winding downhill to the second left horseshoe bend and posted junction at 1.8 miles. The road continues downhill to the Pico Blanco Boy Scout Camp (Hike 18). Leave the road and take the Little Sur River Camp Trail to the right. The narrow footpath winds down the hillside past mossy tree trunks under the shade of oaks and fir. The trail gradually descends one mile by way of eight switchbacks, ending at the streamside Little Sur River Camp.

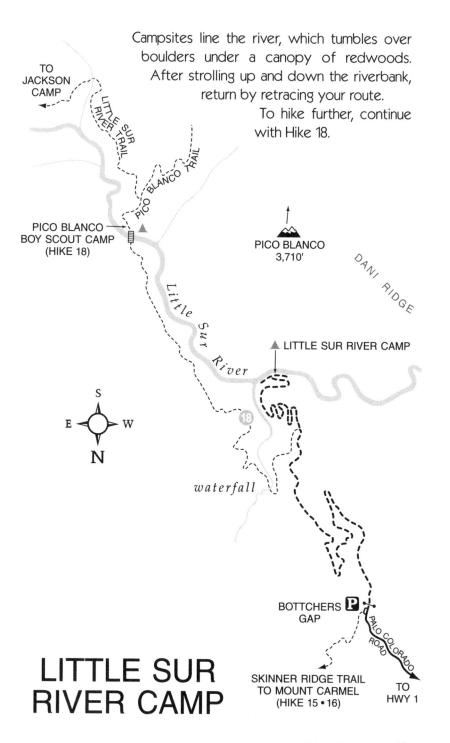

Campsites line the river, which tumbles over boulders under a canopy of redwoods. After strolling up and down the riverbank, return by retracing your route.

To hike further, continue with Hike 18.

TO JACKSON CAMP

LITTLE SUR RIVER TRAIL

PICO BLANCO TRAIL

PICO BLANCO BOY SCOUT CAMP (HIKE 18)

PICO BLANCO 3,710'

DANI RIDGE

Little Sur River

LITTLE SUR RIVER CAMP

S

E ✦ W

N

18

waterfall

BOTTCHERS GAP

PALO COLORADO ROAD

SKINNER RIDGE TRAIL TO MOUNT CARMEL (HIKE 15 • 16)

TO HWY 1

LITTLE SUR RIVER CAMP

Hike 18
Pico Blanco Road to Little Sur River

Hiking distance: 7.2 miles round trip
Hiking time: 3.5 hours
Elevation gain: 1,200 feet
Maps: U.S.G.S. Big Sur
Ventana Wilderness Map

Summary of hike: Pico Blanco Road is an unpaved vehicle-restricted road that winds through the mountains under the shadow of Pico Blanco. The road parallels and descends to the Little Sur River. The road starts from Bottchers Gap at an elevation of 2,050 feet and descends 1,100 feet to a bridge crossing the river at Pico Blanco Boy Scout Camp. The camp was donated to the boy scouts by William Randolph Hearst in 1948. Redwoods planted between 1910 and 1921 surround the camp. The road is on private land with a right-of-way for hikers.

Driving directions: Same as Hike 17.

Hiking directions: From the lower end of the parking lot, pass the locked gate, and head down the unpaved Pico Blanco Road. Descend down the winding mountain road past several magnificent close-up views of Pico Blanco, Dani Ridge and the Pacific Ocean. At 1.8 miles, on a left horseshoe bend, is the posted junction with the Little Sur River Camp Trail on the right (Hike 17). Stay on the road and continue downhill through a redwood forest. Pass a tributary stream with a 15-foot waterfall dropping off a vertical rock ledge. After the stream, the road enters the boy scout property. Stay on the road parallel to the creek, passing a couple of cabins. Pass another group of cabins by the main lodge. At the river, cross the long wooden footbridge, and follow the trail signs to the posted Pico Blanco Trail at the camp crossroads. The Pico Blanco Trail leads up the hill to a trail fork with the Little Sur River Trail. This is our turnaround spot.

To extend the hike, the left fork leads 0.7 miles to Jackson

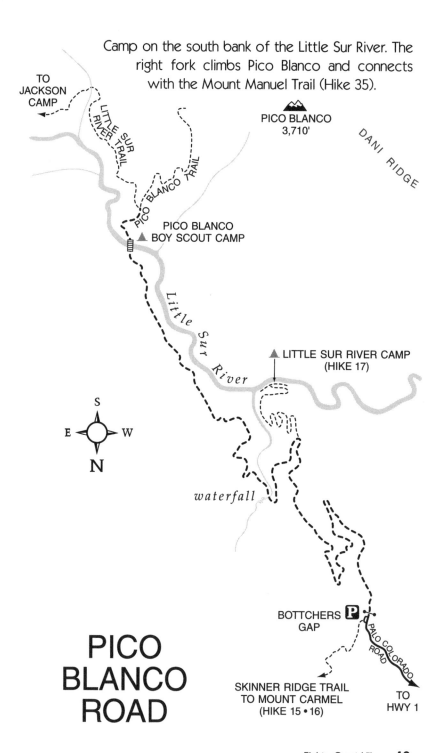

Camp on the south bank of the Little Sur River. The right fork climbs Pico Blanco and connects with the Mount Manuel Trail (Hike 35).

TO JACKSON CAMP

LITTLE SUR RIVER TRAIL

PICO BLANCO TRAIL

PICO BLANCO 3,710'

DANI RIDGE

PICO BLANCO BOY SCOUT CAMP

Little Sur River

LITTLE SUR RIVER CAMP (HIKE 17)

S
E ⊕ W
N

waterfall

BOTTCHERS GAP

PALO COLORADO ROAD

PICO BLANCO ROAD

SKINNER RIDGE TRAIL TO MOUNT CARMEL (HIKE 15 • 16)

TO HWY 1

Hike 19
Old Coast Road—Northern Access

Hiking distance: 11.5 miles round trip (10.2 mile shuttle)
Hiking time: 5.5 hours
Elevation gain: 2,000 feet
Maps: U.S.G.S. Point Sur and Big Sur

map
next page

Summary of hike: The Old Coast Road was the original coastal route connecting Carmel with Big Sur before the Bixby Bridge was completed in 1932. The hike begins at Bixby Bridge and follows the twisting unpaved back road through a shaded canyon dense with coastal redwoods and lush ferns. The trail parallels Bixby Creek and Sierra Creek and crosses two bridges over the Little Sur River. The road is open to the public but is bordered by private property. The hike may be combined with Hike 20 for a 10.2-mile shuttle hike.

Driving directions: From Highway 1 and Rio Road in Carmel, drive 12.7 miles south on Highway 1 to Bixby Bridge. The parking pullout is at the north end of the bridge on the ocean side of the highway.

From the Big Sur Ranger Station, drive 13.5 miles north to the parking pullouts across Bixby Bridge.

Hiking directions: From the north end of Bixby Bridge, take the signed Coast Road inland along the north side of Bixby Creek. At 0.3 miles, as the road curves right, is a great view down canyon of Bixby Bridge and the offshore rocks. Curve south and descend to the canyon floor. Cross a bridge over Bixby Creek. Gently ascend the lower reaches of Sierra Hill along the west wall of the canyon, passing homes tucked into the trees and numerous cliffside tributary streams. As you continue south through a lush redwood forest, Bixby Creek curves away to the east, and the road parallels Sierra Creek, a tributary of Bixby Creek. The road crosses the creek five consecutive times. At the sixth crossing, leave Sierra Creek on a hairpin right bend. Climb out of the shaded canyon to open rolling hillsides on the summit of the Sierra Grade. Descend 1,000 feet along the contours of the mountains on the chaparral slopes of the Sierra Grade. Pico Blanco, at 3,710 feet, dominates the views to the southeast. At the bottom of the grade, walk through a stand of bishop pines to the Little Sur River. Two consecutive metal bridges cross the South Fork and Main Fork Little Sur River just above the confluence. Return along the same trail, or continue with Hike 20 for a one-way shuttle hike.

Hike 20
Old Coast Road—Southern Access

Hiking distance: 9 miles round trip (10.2 mile shuttle)
Hiking time: 4 hours
Elevation gain: 1,650 feet
Maps: U.S.G.S. Big Sur

map
next page

Summary of hike: The Old Coast Road was the primary route of travel along this mountainous coastal stretch prior to 1932 when the Bixby Bridge was opened. This hike begins at the north end of the Big Sur Valley in Andrew Molera State Park near the mouth of the Big Sur River. The winding and breathtaking route curves along hillsides with panoramic vistas of the coastline and interior mountains. The road slowly descends into a shaded canyon, rich with lush ferns and coastal redwoods, to the Little Sur River. The road is open to the public but the adjacent land is privately owned. The hike may be combined with Hike 19 for a 10.2-mile shuttle hike.

Driving directions: From Highway 1 and Rio Road in Carmel, drive 21.4 miles south on Highway 1 to the signed Andrew Molera State Park entrance. Turn right and drive down to the entrance kiosk and parking lot. A parking fee is required.
   From the Big Sur Ranger Station, drive 4.8 miles north to the state park entrance and turn left.

Hiking directions: Walk back up to Highway 1, and cross the highway to the signed Coast Road. Head up the winding, unpaved road on a northern course to steadily improving coastal views. At 1.5 miles, weave through groves of oaks, sycamores and redwoods, reaching the 942-foot summit. Views extend to the coastal marine terrace, Andrew Molera State Park, inland to the South Fork Canyon, and across Dani

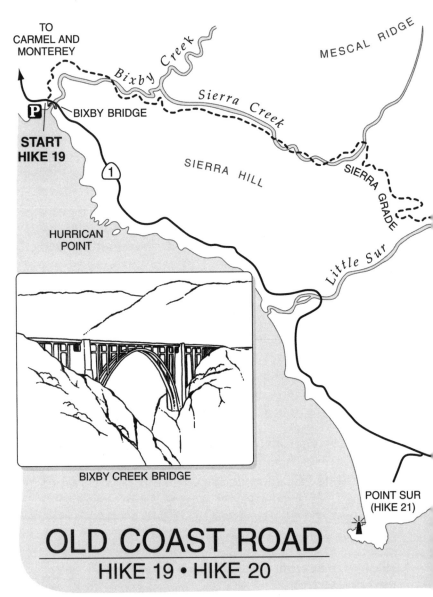

BIXBY CREEK BRIDGE

OLD COAST ROAD
HIKE 19 • HIKE 20

Ridge to the towering 3,710-foot Pico Blanco in the east. Slowly descend, passing a ranch on the left, and enter a lush redwood forest. Skirt around the west edge of Dani Ridge. Parallel the South Fork Little Sur River down the narrow, shaded canyon through oaks, maples, pines, redwoods and an understory of ferns. At the canyon floor, two consecutive metal bridges cross the South Fork and Main Fork Little Sur River just above the confluence. Return along the same trail or continue with Hike 19 for a one-way shuttle hike.

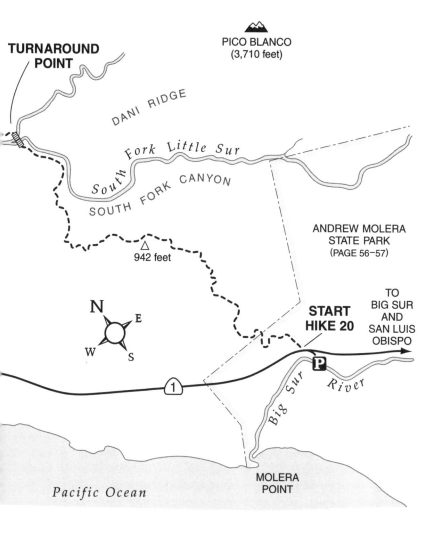

Hike 21
Point Sur Lightstation State Historic Park
Docent led hike: call for scheduled tour times (831) 625-4419

Hiking distance: 1 mile round trip
Hiking time: 3 hours
Elevation gain: 360 feet
Maps: U.S.G.S. Point Sur

Summary of hike: Point Sur is a 361-foot offshore metamorphous rock that is connected to the mainland by a sand bar called a tombolo. The El Sur Ranch owns the surrounding land except for the 34-acre volcanic rock. The Point Sur Lightstation atop the rock was built in 1889. This docent-led hike follows an old horse and buggy route used in the 1800s. The trail overlooks massive offshore rocks and crashing surf. The tour climbs the spiral staircase to the lamp tower at the top of the 38-foot stone lightstation, with panoramic ocean and mountain views from 270 feet. Atop the summit are intact sandstone buildings, restored historic barns and a visitor center.

Driving directions: From Highway 1 and Rio Road in Carmel, drive 18.6 miles south on Highway 1 to the signed Point Sur Lightstation entrance. Park in the pullout along the right side of the highway. A docent will lead a car caravan into the gated property. The base of Point Sur is 0.7 miles ahead. A tour fee is required.

From the Big Sur Ranger Station, drive 7.6 miles north to the Point Sur Lightstation entrance road.

Hiking directions: Ascend the hill on the paved lighthouse road, following the tour guide. The road steadily climbs and curves, overlooking the jagged coastline. Dramatic rocks with crashing whitewater are just offshore. Part of the trail follows an old railway route along the steep cliff. At the lightstation, a spiral staircase leads to the lamp and catwalk. A long set of wooden steps heads up to a ridge and an overlook of the light beacon. The old road leads past a blacksmith and carpenter shop, restored barn, two-foot thick sandstone buildings (once home to lighthouse keepers) and a visitor center at the top of Point Sur. After savoring the magnificent views, return to the parking lot.

POINT SUR

LIGHTSTATION

W

S — N

E

P

TO
MONTEREY

1

TO
BIG SUR

POINT SUR LIGHTSTATION

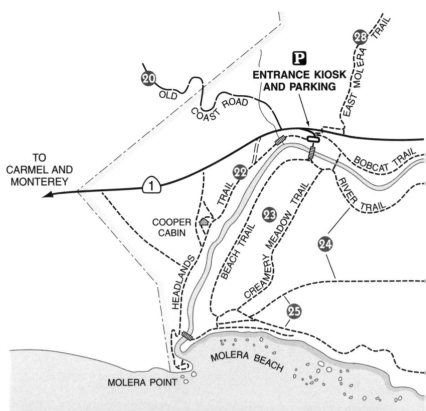

Andrew Molera State Park, the largest state park on the Big Sur coast, encompasses 4,800 acres and extends along both sides of Highway 1. The park has mountains, meadows, a 2.5-mile strand of beach and over 15 miles of hiking trails. The Big Sur River flows through the park.

Driving directions: All of the hikes in this park begin from the parking lot (noted above). From Highway 1 and Rio Road in Carmel, drive 21.4 miles south on Highway 1 to the signed Andrew Molera State Park entrance. Turn right and drive down to the entrance kiosk and parking lot. A parking fee is required. (Some of the trails are also accessible from several gates along Highway 1, which may involve wading through the river.)

From the Big Sur Ranger Station, drive 4.8 miles north to the state park entrance and turn left.

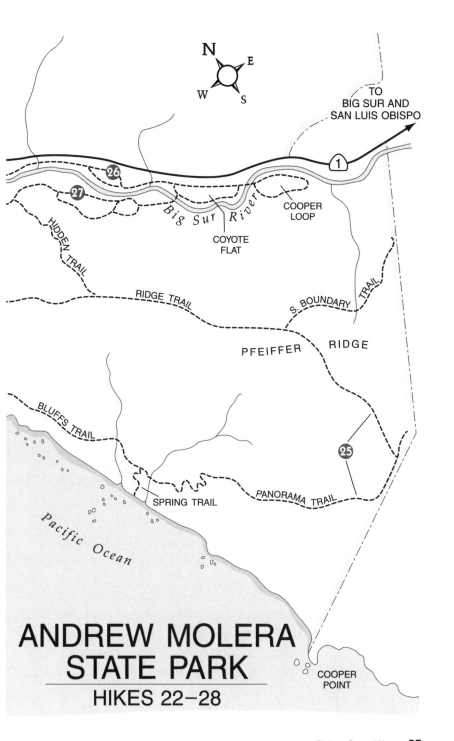

N **E**
W **S**

TO
BIG SUR AND
SAN LUIS OBISPO

1

COOPER
LOOP

Big Sur River

COYOTE
FLAT

HIDDEN TRAIL

RIDGE TRAIL

S. BOUNDARY TRAIL

PFEIFFER RIDGE

BLUFFS TRAIL

25

SPRING TRAIL

PANORAMA TRAIL

Pacific Ocean

ANDREW MOLERA STATE PARK
HIKES 22–28

COOPER
POINT

Hike 22
Headlands Trail to Molera Point
Andrew Molera State Park

Hiking distance: 2.5 miles round trip
Hiking time: 1.5 hours
Elevation gain: 70 feet
Maps: U.S.G.S. Big Sur
         Andrew Molera State Park map

Summary of hike: The Headlands Trail ascends and circles ocean bluffs and Molera Point in Andrew Molera State Park. From the ridge are views of this diverse park, its numerous hiking trails, Molera Beach, the Point Sur Lighthouse and Cooper Point at the south end of the bay. The trail follows the Big Sur River past Cooper Cabin. Built with redwood logs in 1861, the cabin is the oldest surviving ranch structure in Big Sur.

Driving directions: From Highway 1 and Rio Road in Carmel, drive 21.4 miles south on Highway 1 to the signed Andrew Molera State Park entrance. Turn right and drive down to the entrance kiosk and parking lot. A parking fee is required.

From the Big Sur Ranger Station, drive 4.8 miles north to the state park entrance and turn left.

Hiking directions: The signed trail is at the far (northwest) end of the parking lot. Walk past the "Trail Camp" sign and up into a shady grove. Cross a footbridge over a tributary stream, and parallel the Big Sur River. At 0.3 miles, the trail merges with an old ranch road. Bear left, entering Trail Camp, and walk through the campground past large oaks and sycamores. Cooper Cabin is to the south in a eucalyptus grove. After viewing the historic cabin, continue southwest on the ranch road, following the river to a signed junction and map at one mile. The left fork leads to a seasonal bridge crossing the Big Sur River to Molera Beach. Take the right fork on the Headlands Trail up wooden steps to the ridge. Walk out to sea on the headlands, circling the point. Return by reversing your route.

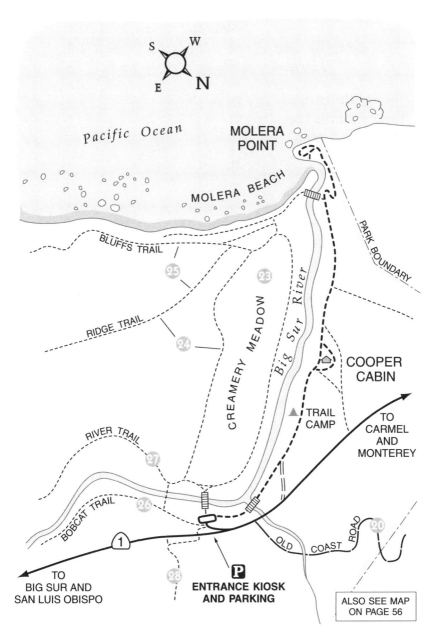

Pacific Ocean

MOLERA POINT

MOLERA BEACH

BLUFFS TRAIL

RIDGE TRAIL

CREAMERY MEADOW

Big Sur River

PARK BOUNDARY

COOPER CABIN

TRAIL CAMP

TO CARMEL AND MONTEREY

RIVER TRAIL

BOBCAT TRAIL

OLD COAST ROAD

TO BIG SUR AND SAN LUIS OBISPO

P
ENTRANCE KIOSK AND PARKING

ALSO SEE MAP ON PAGE 56

HEADSLANDS TRAIL
MOLERA POINT

Hike 23
Creamery Meadow—Molera Beach Loop
Andrew Molera State Park

Hiking distance: 2 mile loop
Hiking time: 1 hour
Elevation gain: Level
Maps: U.S.G.S. Big Sur
       Andrew Molera State Park map

Summary of hike: This is an easy, level hike to Molera Beach in Andrew Molera State Park. The loop hike meanders through a grassy meadow lined with sycamore trees and returns parallel to the Big Sur River. Molera Beach sits below Molera Point and the headlands (Hike 22). Although the beach extends south for two miles, the tide often makes further access impossible.

Driving directions: Follow the driving directions from the Andrew Molera State Park map on page 56.

Hiking directions: Cross the seasonal footbridge over the Big Sur River, or wade across if removed, to a trail split. The Beach Trail, our return route, bears right. Begin the loop to the left on the River Trail to a second junction 50 yards ahead. Again bear left, staying on the River Trail to a third junction. Take the Creamery Meadow Trail to the right, following the base of the hillside along the edge of the meadow. Pass the Ridge Trail on the left (Hike 24) to a junction with the Beach Trail at 0.9 miles, our return route. Bear left on the Beach Trail along the Big Sur River to the back of the sand beach. The Bluffs Trail (Hike 25) heads uphill to the left. Continue straight to the sandy shoreline. To the northwest, the beach ends at the mouth of the Big Sur River along the base of Molera Point and the Headland Bluffs (Hike 22). After exploring the beach, return to the junction with the Creamery Meadow Trail. Stay left on the Beach Trail and follow the river upstream a short distance. Soon the river veers left, and the footpath curves through the grassy meadow dotted with sycamore and cottonwood trees. The trail is separated from the river by dense willow thickets. Meander through Creamery Meadow, completing the loop near the river. Return to the left.

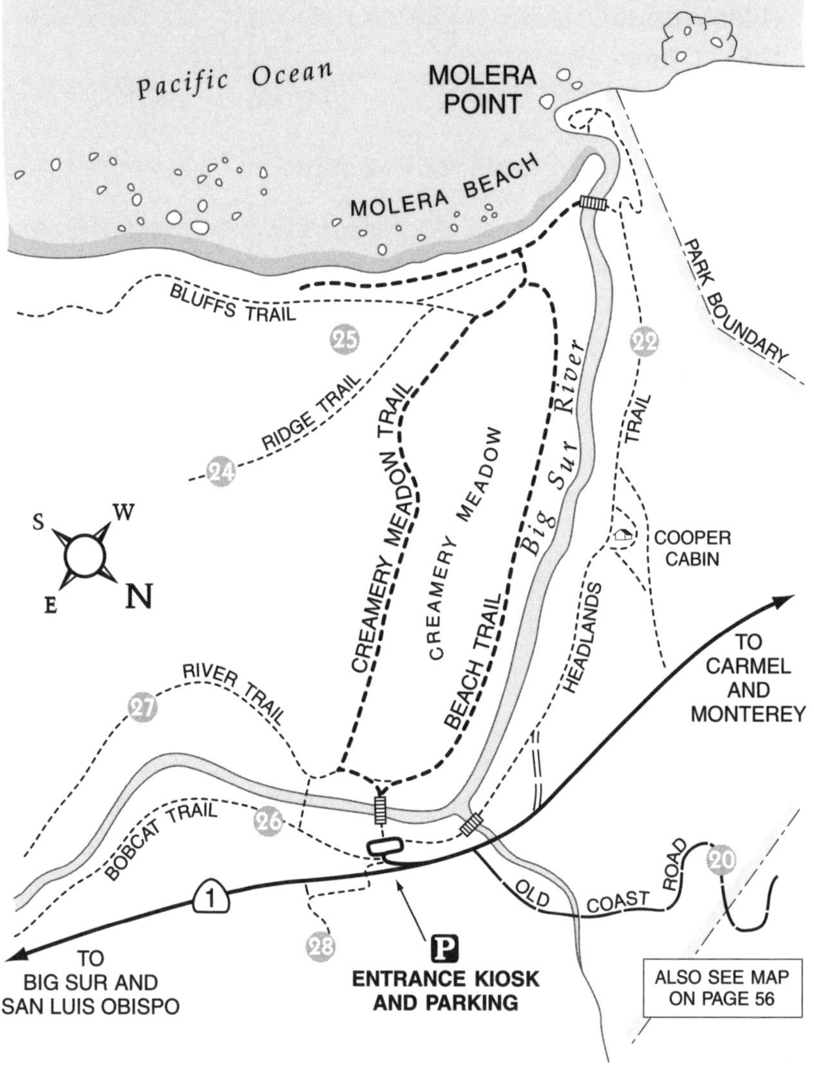

Pacific Ocean

MOLERA POINT

MOLERA BEACH

PARK BOUNDARY

BLUFFS TRAIL

25

RIDGE TRAIL

24

22

CREAMERY MEADOW TRAIL

CREAMERY MEADOW

BEACH TRAIL

Big Sur River

TRAIL

COOPER CABIN

HEADLANDS

S W

E N

RIVER TRAIL

27

TO CARMEL AND MONTEREY

BOBCAT TRAIL

26

20

1

OLD COAST ROAD

28

TO BIG SUR AND SAN LUIS OBISPO

P
ENTRANCE KIOSK AND PARKING

ALSO SEE MAP ON PAGE 56

CREAMERY MEADOW
MOLERA BEACH

Hike 24
Ridge Trail—Hidden Trail—River Trail Loop
Andrew Molera State Park

Hiking distance: 3.6 mile loop
Hiking time: 2 hours
Elevation gain: 700 feet
Maps: U.S.G.S. Big Sur
　　　　Andrew Molera State Park map

Summary of hike: This loop hike follows the Big Sur River upstream to Hidden Trail. The trail climbs 570 feet, winding in and out of shady live oak glens and grassy coyote brush slopes, to Pfeiffer Ridge (Molera Ridge). From the ridge are 360-degree panoramic views of the crenulated coastline, Point Sur, the Big Sur River canyon, Mount Manuel and Pico Blanco. The path follows the ridge, the backbone of Andrew Molera State Park, down to Creamery Meadow.

Driving directions: Follow the driving directions from the Andrew Molera State Park map on page 56.

Hiking directions: Take the posted Beach Trail across the Big Sur River to a trail split. (If the summer footbridge has been removed, wade across.) Follow the River Trail, bearing left at two consecutive junctions, to the foot of the hill and a trail split. The Creamery Meadow Trail goes to the right (Hike 23). Stay on the River Trail to the left, and curve right around the base of the hillside, following the Big Sur River upstream. Skirt the west edge of the meadow along the foot of the hillside. The path gains elevation through an oak canopy to the posted junction on the right. Take the Hidden Trail to the right and ascend the hill, alternating between oak groves and small open meadows. Cross a two-plank bridge over a small gulch to the open chaparral. Along the Big Sur River below are distinct groves of redwoods towering above the oaks and pines. Along the trail, wooden steps aid in footing and curb erosion. The 0.7-mile Hidden Trail ends at a posted T-junction with the Ridge

Trail. The left fork follows Pfeiffer Ridge to the 1,050-foot summit (Hike 25). Take the right fork, following the ridge up a short hill to a level flat at 703 feet. There are grand coastal vistas of Molera Point and the Point Sur Lightstation. Descend along the seaward ridge, overlooking the state park, to a 3-way junction on a flat at the ridge bottom. The left fork follows the Bluffs Trail south (Hike 25). Take the right fork, dropping into Creamery Meadow. Bear right along the south edge of the meadow, contouring the base of the hillside and completing the loop at the River Trail. Retrace your steps to the left.

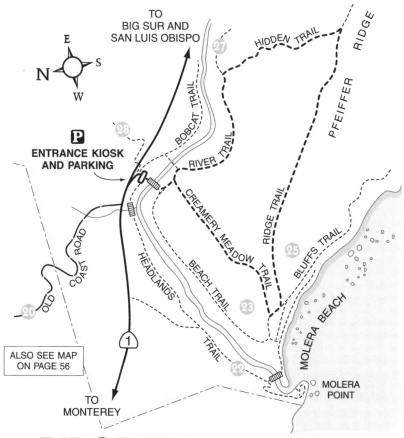

RIDGE TRAIL • HIDDEN TRAIL • RIVER TRAIL

Hike 25
Bluffs—Panorama—Ridge Loop
Andrew Molera State Park

Hiking distance: 9 mile loop
Hiking time: 4.5 hours
Elevation gain: 1,100 feet
Maps: U.S.G.S. Big Sur
        Andrew Molera State Park map

Summary of hike: This hike circles the western side of Andrew Molera State Park through a diverse cross-section of landscape that includes coastal bluffs, isolated beach coves, forested stream canyons, redwood forests, mountain top overlooks, meadows and a river crossing. The long loop trail meanders for two miles on the flat marine terrace, then climbs up a ridge at the south park boundary to sweeping coastal and mountain views. The trail descends along Pfeiffer Ridge through oak forests, massive redwood groves and open grasslands with vistas of the Big Sur coastline.

Driving directions: Follow the driving directions from the Andrew Molera State Park map on page 56.

Hiking directions: At the signed Beach Trail near the middle of the parking lot, cross the Big Sur River on the summer footbridge (or wade across if removed) to a trail fork. Stay to the left on the River Trail. Bear left again fifty yards ahead, staying on the River Trail to a posted junction at the base of the hillside. The River Trail curves left. Take the Creamery Meadow Trail right, and contour southwest along the base of the hill, skirting the edge of the meadow. At 0.8 miles is a junction with the Ridge Trail on the left. Leave the meadow and head up the ridge to an open flat and trail fork. Begin the loop to the right on the Bluffs Trail. Cross the wide marine terrace between the jagged coastal cliffs and the inland hills. Pass several side paths that lead to the edge of the cliffs. Curve around a pair of eroding, spring-fed gullies. Dip in and out of another gulch to the end of the

Bluffs Trail at a posted trail junction. The Spring Trail bears right, and zigzags down a draw to a small pocket beach. Continue on the Panorama Trail, dropping into a drainage. Climb out and steadily wind up the hillside to the park's south boundary and views of Pacific Valley and the Big Sur coast. Curve along the fenced boundary to the end of the Panorama Trail on the summit at 4.6 miles. A bench, set among the cypress trees, offers a respite with sweeping coastal views. Take the posted Ridge Trail north, descending towards the towering redwoods ahead. The spongy, needle-covered path levels out and meanders through a shady grove of massive redwoods and twisted oaks draped with lace lichen. Pass the South Boundary Trail on the right, and follow Pfeiffer Ridge across the exposed grass and chaparral. Cross two long sweeping saddles to a junction with Hidden Trail. Continue down the seaward ridge, completing the loop at the base of the ridge on the Bluffs Trail.

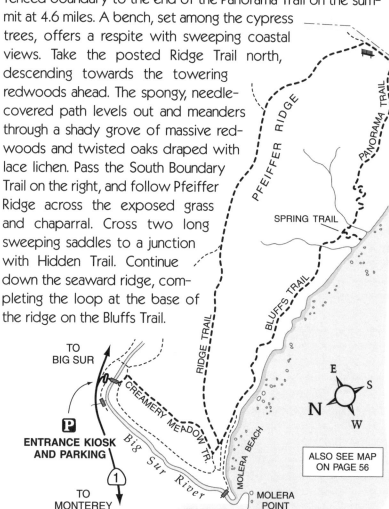

BLUFFS TRAIL • PANORAMA TRAIL • RIDGE TRAIL

Hike 26
Bobcat Trail to Coyote Flat
Andrew Molera State Park

Hiking distance: 4.5 miles round trip
Hiking time: 2 hours
Elevation gain: Level
Maps: U.S.G.S. Big Sur
     Andrew Molera State Park map

Summary of hike: The Big Sur River flows through Andrew Molera State Park and empties into the Pacific at Molera Beach. The near-level Bobcat Trail parallels the east bank of the Big Sur River, meandering through redwood groves and lush carpets of ferns. The trail crosses small seasonal streams and loops through two meadows.

Driving directions: Follow the driving directions from the Andrew Molera State Park map on page 56.

Hiking directions: Walk back to the entrance of the parking lot. Ten yards past the kiosk, take the unpaved Ranch House road to the right. Follow the road southeast through oak and maple groves, passing a river crossing on the right and barns on the left. At the far (south) end of the corrals, the road ends at the posted Bobcat Trail on the right. Take the footpath through a shady grove lush with ferns, poison oak and towering redwoods. Weave through the forest between the Big Sur River and Highway 1, passing a trail access from Highway 1. Curve away from the highway to an open meadow. A path loops around the perimeter of the meadow. Take the right fork along the west edge of the meadow. Beyond the meadow, the trail descends to a small sandy beach by a rock cliff on the banks of the Big Sur River. Across the river is River Trail—the return route for Hike 27. Follow the watercourse upstream, cross a tributary stream, and wind through a redwood grove to a Y-fork. Curve right and descend into Coyote Flat and a trail split. Again a trail circles the large meadow. Take the right fork along the south-

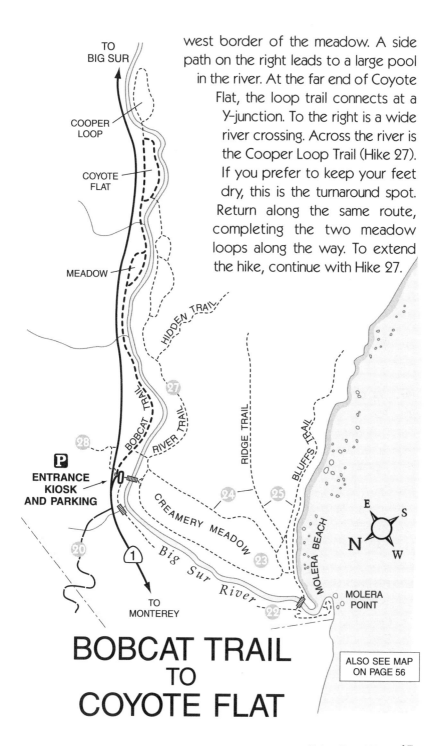

west border of the meadow. A side path on the right leads to a large pool in the river. At the far end of Coyote Flat, the loop trail connects at a Y-junction. To the right is a wide river crossing. Across the river is the Cooper Loop Trail (Hike 27). If you prefer to keep your feet dry, this is the turnaround spot. Return along the same route, completing the two meadow loops along the way. To extend the hike, continue with Hike 27.

TO BIG SUR

COOPER LOOP

COYOTE FLAT

MEADOW

HIDDEN TRAIL

BOBCAT TRAIL

RIVER TRAIL

RIDGE TRAIL

BLUFFS TRAIL

P
ENTRANCE KIOSK AND PARKING

CREAMERY MEADOW

MOLERA BEACH

Big Sur River

1

TO MONTEREY

MOLERA POINT

E
N · S · W

BOBCAT TRAIL
TO
COYOTE FLAT

ALSO SEE MAP ON PAGE 56

Hike 27
Bobcat—River Loop
Andrew Molera State Park

Hiking distance: 5 mile loop
Hiking time: 2.5 hours
Elevation gain: 50 feet
Maps: U.S.G.S. Big Sur
　　　　Andrew Molera State Park map

Summary of hike: The Bobcat and River trails loop around the east and west banks of the Big Sur River in Andrew Molera State Park. The route crosses four meadows, winds through numerous redwood groves, passes a few swimming holes and crosses the Big Sur River four times.

Driving directions: Follow the driving directions from the Andrew Molera State Park map on page 56.

Hiking directions: Begin at the end of the previous hike—the Bobcat Trail/Hike 26—on the end of Coyote Flat at the edge of the Big Sur River. Wade across the river to a trail fork. The Cooper Loop may be hiked in either direction. This route begins on the left fork, hiking clockwise. Wind through the thick forest to the banks of the river. Follow the river upstream to the far end of the loop. Curve right, leaving the river, and enter a dense redwood grove with lush ferns. Complete the 0.7-mile loop, and cross the river again. Return through Coyote Flat, taking the right fork this time around the east end of the meadow. Pass a highway access trail on the right. Beyond Coyote Flat, descend through redwoods, crossing a tributary stream to a small pocket beach at the river by rock cliffs. Wade across the river to the west bank, and pick up the unsigned River Trail. Stay to the right on the route closest to the river, passing open meadows dotted with trees and views of the surrounding mountains. Skirt the west side of the meadow along the base of the cliffs. Curve left up a small rise, passing a junction with the Hidden Trail on the left. Gradually descend back to the

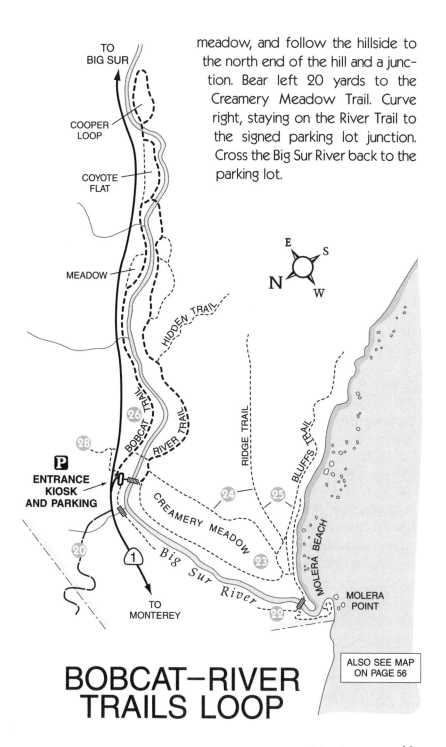

meadow, and follow the hillside to the north end of the hill and a junction. Bear left 20 yards to the Creamery Meadow Trail. Curve right, staying on the River Trail to the signed parking lot junction. Cross the Big Sur River back to the parking lot.

TO BIG SUR

COOPER LOOP

COYOTE FLAT

MEADOW

HIDDEN TRAIL

BOBCAT TRAIL

RIVER TRAIL

RIDGE TRAIL

BLUFFS TRAIL

P
ENTRANCE KIOSK AND PARKING

CREAMERY MEADOW

MOLERA BEACH

1

Big Sur River

TO MONTEREY

MOLERA POINT

E S N W

BOBCAT–RIVER TRAILS LOOP

ALSO SEE MAP ON PAGE 56

Hike 28
East Molera Trail
Andrew Molera State Park

Hiking distance: 4 miles round trip
Hiking time: 2 hours
Elevation gain: 1,500 feet
Maps: U.S.G.S. Big Sur
Andrew Molera State Park map

Summary of hike: Andrew Molera State Park encompasses 4,800 acres along both sides of Highway 1, with the majority of the acreage east of the highway. The East Molera Trail climbs up the south-facing slope of the Santa Lucia Mountains to panoramic vistas of the entire state park and beyond. The path crosses an old cattle grazing pasture to a ridge, where there is a beautiful grove of stately redwoods backed by towering Pico Blanco. The views include Molera Beach, Molera Point, Creamery Meadow, the Big Sur River, Trail Camp, Pfeiffer Ridge and the Point Sur Lightstation.

Driving directions: Follow the driving directions from the Andrew Molera State Park map on page 56.

Hiking directions: Walk past the entrance kiosk and up the road to the left bend. Bear right on the unpaved road, marked "Authorized Personnel Only," a short distance to the signed East Molera Trail on the left. Take the footpath uphill and through the tunnel under Highway 1. At 0.2 miles is a signed junction. To the right is the highway access. Bear left uphill through a shady oak grove to an old ranch road. Follow the forested road to the left, passing a water tank on the right. The trail emerges from the forest canopy to the open sloping grassland. Cross the slopes to the southern edge of the ridge. Veer left and traverse the west face of the mountain. Continue up two long sweeping switchbacks. Wind around the south side of the mountain to the head of the canyon and a beautiful stand of redwoods on the ridge. Across the inland canyon is pyramid-shaped Pico Blanco and the South Fork Little Sur River canyon. A path follows the ridge in both directions. To the right are stately oaks and views up the Big Sur Valley. To the left is the summit and awesome coastal views. After marveling at the vistas, return along the same route.

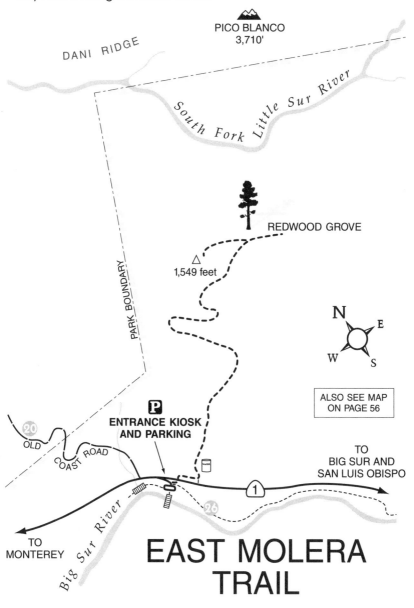

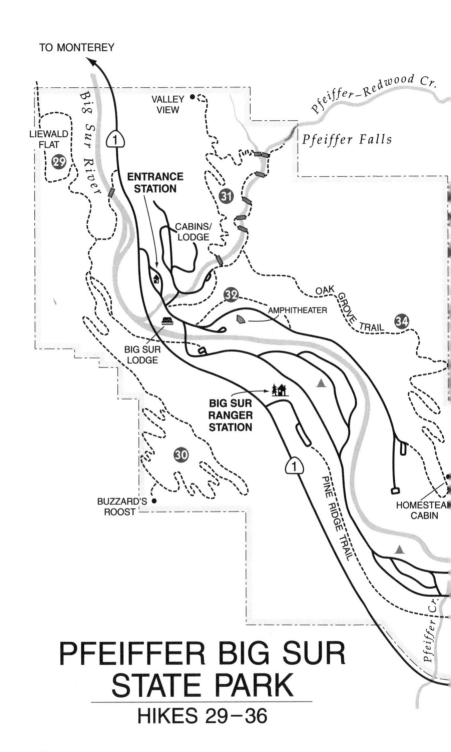

TO MONTEREY

Big Sur River

VALLEY VIEW

Pfeiffer–Redwood Cr.

Pfeiffer Falls

LIEWALD FLAT

29

1

ENTRANCE STATION

CABINS/ LODGE

31

32

OAK GROVE TRAIL

34

AMPHITHEATER

BIG SUR LODGE

BIG SUR RANGER STATION

30

BUZZARD'S ROOST

1

PINE RIDGE TRAIL

HOMESTEAD CABIN

Pfeiffer Cr.

PFEIFFER BIG SUR STATE PARK
HIKES 29–36

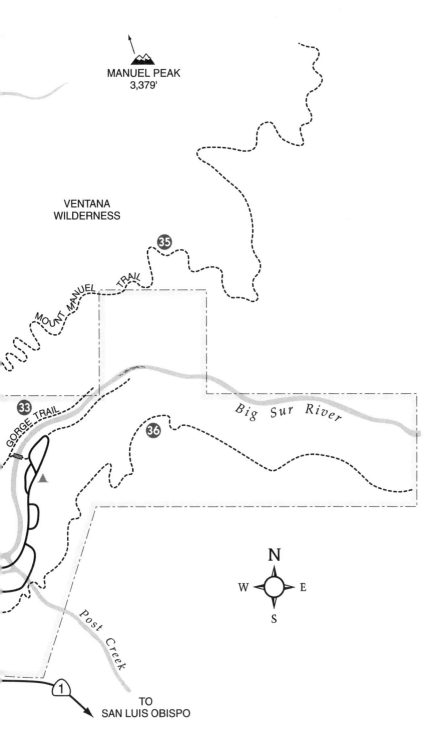

MANUEL PEAK
3,379'

VENTANA
WILDERNESS

35

MOUNT MANUEL TRAIL

GORGE TRAIL

33

36

Big Sur River

Post Creek

N
W — E
S

1 TO
SAN LUIS OBISPO

Hike 29
Liewald Flat
Pfeiffer Big Sur State Park

Hiking distance: 1.6 miles round trip
Hiking time: 1 hour
Elevation gain: 200 feet
Maps: U.S.G.S. Big Sur and Pfeiffer Point
      Pfeiffer Big Sur State Park map

Summary of hike: Liewald Flat is an oval-shaped meadow dotted with oak trees and rimmed with pines in Pfeiffer Big Sur State Park. The trail to the flat follows an old road parallel to the Big Sur River. The meandering path winds through a quiet pastoral forest with large old growth redwood trees, oaks and bay laurels.

Driving directions: From the Big Sur Ranger Station, located 27 miles south of Carmel, drive 0.5 miles north on Highway 1 to the signed Pfeiffer Big Sur State Park entrance. Turn right (inland) past the entrance station to the stop sign. Continue straight through the intersection, and turn right just after passing the Big Sur Lodge on the right. Drive 0.1 mile, crossing a bridge over the Big Sur River and curving left to the trailhead parking area on the left. An entrance fee is required.

Hiking directions: Hike past the trail sign, and cross under the bridge spanning the Big Sur River. Head downstream and cross under Highway 1. Follow the river past huge redwoods in the shady forest to an unsigned junction. The left fork gently ascends the hillside. The right fork stays close to the river and climbs steps, where the two forks rejoin. A short distance ahead is the signed Buzzard's Roost Trail on the left (Hike 30). Go straight on the main trail, high above the Big Sur River, to a T-junction at the group campground. The right fork leads through the campground. Take the left fork on the old road above the campground. The trail emerges from the dense forest into Liewald Flat, an open meadow with oak groves. Begin the loop around the meadow to the right. At the far (north) end of the meadow, an unsigned footpath veers to the right into the forest. Stay on the main path and continue above the meadow, completing the loop. Return along the same route.

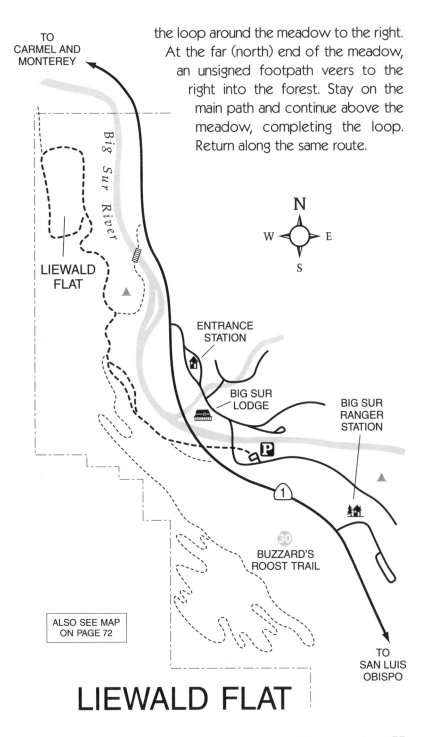

TO
CARMEL AND
MONTEREY

Big Sur River

LIEWALD
FLAT

N
W E
S

ENTRANCE
STATION

BIG SUR
LODGE

BIG SUR
RANGER
STATION

P

1

30
BUZZARD'S
ROOST TRAIL

ALSO SEE MAP
ON PAGE 72

TO
SAN LUIS
OBISPO

LIEWALD FLAT

Hike 30
Buzzard's Roost
Pfeiffer Big Sur State Park

Hiking distance: 2.5 miles round trip
Hiking time: 1.5 hours
Elevation gain: 800 feet
Maps: U.S.G.S. Big Sur and Pfeiffer Point
 Pfeiffer Big Sur State Park map

Summary of hike: The Buzzard's Roost Trail begins as a streamside stroll along the Big Sur River through groves of bay laurel, oak and huge redwoods. Switchbacks wind up the forested hillside slope to Pfeiffer Ridge, forming a 1.7-mile loop. Manzanita and chaparral line the ridge with far-reaching views of the Santa Lucia Mountains and the Pacific Ocean.

Driving directions: From the Big Sur Ranger Station, located 27 miles south of Carmel, drive 0.5 miles north on Highway 1 to the signed Pfeiffer Big Sur State Park entrance. Turn right (inland) past the entrance station to the stop sign. Continue straight through the intersection, and turn right just after passing the Big Sur Lodge on the right. Drive 0.1 mile, crossing a bridge over the Big Sur River and curving left to the trailhead parking area on the left. An entrance fee is required.

Hiking directions: Take the signed trail, crossing under the bridge that spans the Big Sur River. Follow the river downstream and under Highway 1. Gradually ascend the hillside past redwoods in the shade of the forest. The trail splits and joins a short distance ahead. Traverse the hillside to the signed Buzzard's Roost Trail on the left. The main trail leads to the campground and Liewald Flat (Hike 29). Take the sharp left switchback, and climb up the hillside ledge to a trail split at 0.9 miles. Begin the loop to the left. The path levels out and winds in and out of ravines along the contours of the mountain. Head up more switchbacks to Pfeiffer Ridge, overlooking the Big Sur Valley, Mount Manuel and the Pacific Ocean. Steps lead up the eroded ridge to Buzzard's Roost. A short side path on the left by the antenna structure detours to an overlook. Return to the main trail, and descend the ridge into the forest. Continue weaving down the mountain, completing the loop. Bear left and retrace your steps to the trailhead.

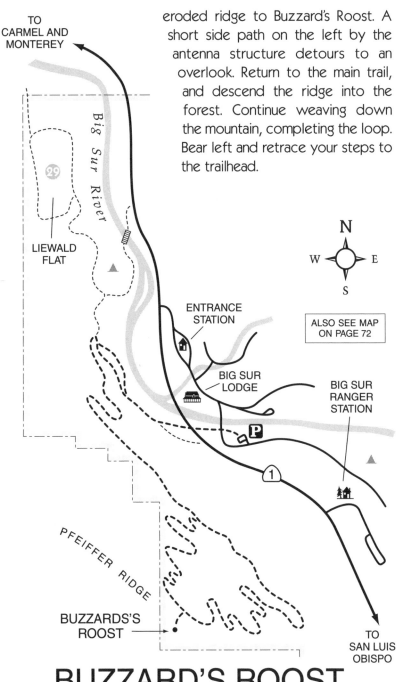

BUZZARD'S ROOST

Hike 31
Pfeiffer Falls—Valley View Loop
Pfeiffer Big Sur State Park

Hiking distance: 2.2 miles round trip
Hiking time: 1 hour
Elevation gain: 450 feet
Maps: U.S.G.S. Big Sur
Pfeiffer Big Sur State Park map

Summary of hike: Pfeiffer Falls spills 60 feet over granite rock in a small fern grotto. The moist, fern-lined trail follows Pfeiffer-Redwood Creek up the canyon through a redwood forest to the base of the falls. On the return, the Valley View Trail climbs out of the canyon into an oak and chaparral woodland. From an overlook are sweeping views of the Santa Lucia Range, the Big Sur Valley, Point Sur and the blue Pacific Ocean.

Driving directions: From the Big Sur Ranger Station, located 27 miles south of Carmel, drive 0.5 miles north on Highway 1 to the signed Pfeiffer Big Sur State Park entrance. Turn right (inland) to the entrance station. Continue to a stop sign. Turn left and a quick right, following the trail signs 0.2 miles to the signed trailhead parking area on the right. An entrance fee is required.

Hiking directions: Take the trail at the far (northeast) end of the parking area. Head gradually uphill through the redwood forest. Parallel Pfeiffer-Redwood Creek to the signed Valley View Trail on the left. Begin the loop to the right. Ascend a long series of steps to a signed junction with the Oak Grove Trail (Hike 34) on the right. Continue up the canyon towards Pfeiffer Falls as the path zigzags upstream over four wooden footbridges. After the fourth crossing is the second junction with the Valley View Trail on the left, the return route. Stay to the right, climbing two sets of stairs to a platform in front of Pfeiffer Falls. Return to the junction and take the Valley View Trail, crossing a bridge over the creek and another bridge over a tributary stream. Switchbacks lead up the south-facing slope to a signed junction. Bear right towards the Valley View Overlook. Ascend the ridge 0.3 miles to a short loop at the overlook. Return downhill to the junction, and bear right to the canyon floor. Cross the bridge over the creek, completing the loop on the Pfeiffer Falls Trail. Return to the trailhead on the right.

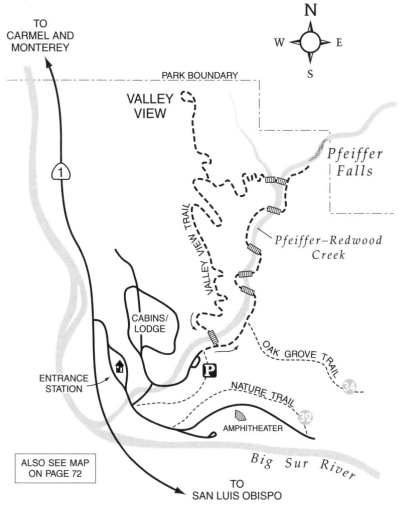

PFEIFFER FALLS–
VALLEY VIEW LOOP

Hike 32
Nature Trail
Pfeiffer Big Sur State Park

Hiking distance: 0.6 miles round trip
Hiking time: 30 minutes
Elevation gain: Level
Maps: U.S.G.S. Big Sur and Pfeiffer Point
      Pfeiffer Big Sur State Park map

Summary of hike: The Nature Trail in Pfeiffer Big Sur State Park is a short self-guiding trail that meanders through a variety of plant life native to the Big Sur area. The pastoral path begins across the park road from the Big Sur River in an oak woodland. The trail ends in a beautiful redwood grove. Interpretive leaflets available at the trailhead describe the surrounding trees, their effects and uses.

Driving directions: From the Big Sur Ranger Station, located 27 miles south of Carmel, drive 0.5 miles north on Highway 1 to the signed Pfeiffer Big Sur State Park entrance. Turn right (inland) past the entrance station to the stop sign. Continue straight through the intersection, passing Big Sur Lodge on the right, 0.3 miles to the picnic and parking area on the right. An entrance fee is required.

You may also begin the trail from the Big Sur Lodge.

Hiking directions: From the grassy picnic area on the banks of the Big Sur River, cross the park road to the signed Nature Trail. Pick up the interpretive guide, and enter the forest of live oaks and sycamores. The level path continues into a lush redwood grove. Wind through the shady grove, and climb a short flight of wooden steps, reaching the park road across from Big Sur Lodge. Return along the same path or the park road.

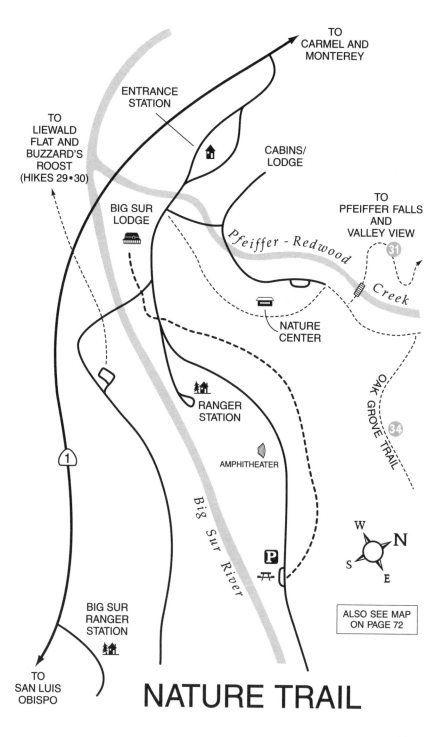

TO CARMEL AND MONTEREY

ENTRANCE STATION

TO LIEWALD FLAT AND BUZZARD'S ROOST (HIKES 29•30)

CABINS/ LODGE

BIG SUR LODGE

TO PFEIFFER FALLS AND VALLEY VIEW

31

Pfeiffer - Redwood

Creek

NATURE CENTER

1

RANGER STATION

OAK GROVE TRAIL

34

AMPHITHEATER

Big Sur River

W N S E

P

BIG SUR RANGER STATION

ALSO SEE MAP ON PAGE 72

TO SAN LUIS OBISPO

NATURE TRAIL

Hike 33
Gorge Trail
Pfeiffer Big Sur State Park

Hiking distance: 1.4 miles round trip
Hiking time: 45 minutes
Elevation gain: 150 feet
Maps: U.S.G.S. Big Sur and Pfeiffer Point
Pfeiffer Big Sur State Park map

Summary of hike: The Gorge Trail leads into a narrow gorge to cascades and several swimming holes on the Big Sur River. The trail follows two short, unmaintained paths bordering the rocky east and west banks of the river. Both root-strewn paths scramble through an undeveloped area adjacent to the cascading whitewater. The headwall of the steep gorge is lush with moss covered rocks and ferns.

Driving directions: From the Big Sur Ranger Station, located 27 miles south of Carmel, drive 0.5 miles north on Highway 1 to the signed Pfeiffer Big Sur State Park entrance. Turn right (inland) past the entrance station to the stop sign. Continue straight through the intersection, passing Big Sur Lodge on the right, and bear left, following the signs towards the picnic area. At 0.7 miles is the signed trailhead parking area on the left. An entrance fee is required.

Hiking directions: Take the gated fire road past the trail sign into the shade of the old oak forest. At 0.1 mile is a junction at the Homestead Cabin, an historic wooden cabin on the left. The Oak Grove Trail (Hike 34) bears left. Take the right fork, staying on the Gorge Trail. Follow the west side of the Big Sur River to the bridge spanning the river. Before crossing the bridge, a unsigned footpath veers left to the northwest bank of the river. This path ends where the river meets the sheer rock canyon walls. Return to the bridge, and cross it into the campground. Follow the campground road left, parallel to the river. As the road curves away from the river, take the well-defined

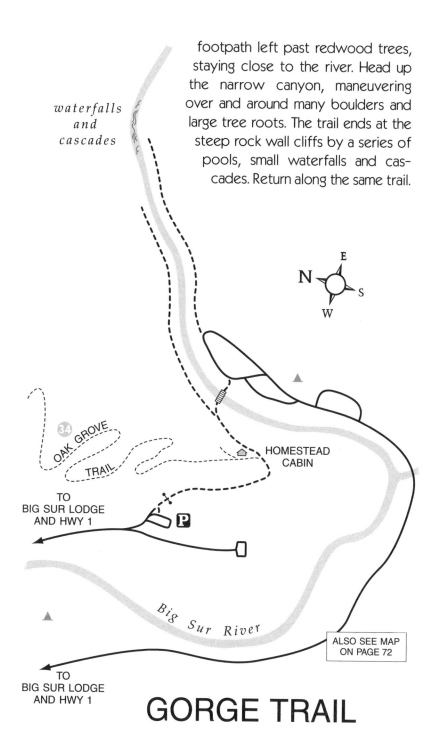

footpath left past redwood trees, staying close to the river. Head up the narrow canyon, maneuvering over and around many boulders and large tree roots. The trail ends at the steep rock wall cliffs by a series of pools, small waterfalls and cascades. Return along the same trail.

waterfalls and cascades

E
N
S
W

OAK GROVE
TRAIL

HOMESTEAD CABIN

TO
BIG SUR LODGE
AND HWY 1

P

Big Sur River

ALSO SEE MAP
ON PAGE 72

TO
BIG SUR LODGE
AND HWY 1

GORGE TRAIL

Hike 34
Oak Grove Trail
Pfeiffer Big Sur State Park

Hiking distance: 2.8 mile loop
Hiking time: 1.5 hours
Elevation gain: 350 feet
Maps: U.S.G.S. Big Sur and Pfeiffer Point
Pfeiffer Big Sur State Park map

Summary of hike: The Oak Grove Trail traverses a beautiful forested hillside through several natural ecosystems. The plant communities range from dry chaparral to hardwood forests and shady redwood groves. The path weaves in and out of numerous gullies, connecting Pfeiffer Falls Trail (Hike 31) with the Gorge Trail. This is also the access route to the Mount Manuel Trail (Hike 35).

Driving directions: From the Big Sur Ranger Station, located 27 miles south of Carmel, drive 0.5 miles north on Highway 1 to the signed Pfeiffer Big Sur State Park entrance. Turn right (inland) past the entrance station to the stop sign. Continue straight through the intersection, passing Big Sur Lodge on the right, and bear left, following the signs towards the picnic area. At 0.7 miles is the signed trailhead parking area on the left. An entrance fee is required.

Hiking directions: Take the gated road past the trail sign into the shade of the old oak forest. At 0.1 mile is a junction at the Homestead Cabin on the left. The right fork follows the Big Sur River along the Gorge Trail (Hike 33). Take the left fork on the Oak Grove Trail to the Homestead Cabin and a trail fork. Keep to the left, straight ahead, through the open coastal oak grove. Switchback up the hillside, alternating between shady oak woodlands to exposed scrub and chaparral. At 0.7 miles, the path levels out on a 560-foot saddle by a signed junction with the Mount Manuel Trail. Stay on the Oak Grove Trail to the left, curving down the oak covered hillside. Descend into a small ravine and cross the drainage on a wooden footbridge, reaching the west end of the trail at a T-junction with the Pfeiffer Falls Trail at 1.7 miles. Bear left through a grove of redwoods, and parallel Pfeiffer-Redwood Creek to the paved park road. Follow the park road downhill and bear left at the lodge. Follow the forested road 0.6 miles back to the parking lot.

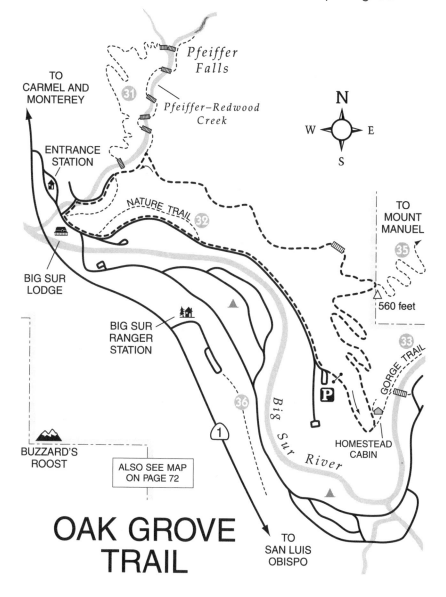

TO
CARMEL AND
MONTEREY

*Pfeiffer
Falls*

*Pfeiffer–Redwood
Creek*

N
W   E
S

ENTRANCE
STATION

NATURE TRAIL

TO
MOUNT
MANUEL

BIG SUR
LODGE

560 feet

BIG SUR
RANGER
STATION

GORGE TRAIL

P

*Big
Sur
River*

HOMESTEAD
CABIN

BUZZARD'S
ROOST

ALSO SEE MAP
ON PAGE 72

1

OAK GROVE
TRAIL

TO
SAN LUIS
OBISPO

Hike 35
Mount Manuel Trail
Pfeiffer Big Sur State Park

Hiking distance: 10.4 miles round trip
Hiking time: 5.5 hours
Elevation gain: 3,200 feet
Maps: U.S.G.S. Big Sur and Pfeiffer Point
Pfeiffer Big Sur State Park map

Summary of hike: Mount Manuel is the towering mountain that dominates Pfeiffer Big Sur State Park. This hike climbs to the vista point near the 3,379-foot summit. The sweeping 360-degree panoramic views extend across the entire Big Sur area, from the Santa Lucia Mountains to the expansive crenelated coastline and sheer coastal cliffs. The trail begins from the Oak Grove Trail—Hike 34. The hike up to the vista point is on exposed chaparral covered hillsides that offer little shade.

Driving directions: From the Big Sur Ranger Station, located 27 miles south of Carmel, drive 0.5 miles north on Highway 1 to the signed Pfeiffer Big Sur State Park entrance. Turn right (inland) past the entrance station to the stop sign. Continue straight through the intersection, passing Big Sur Lodge on the right, and bear left, following the signs towards the picnic area. At 0.7 miles is the signed trailhead parking area on the left. An entrance fee is required.

Hiking directions: Take the gated road past the trail sign into the shade of the old oak forest. At 0.1 mile is a junction at the Homestead Cabin on the left. The right fork follows the Big Sur River along the Gorge Trail (Hike 33). Take the left fork to the Homestead Cabin and a trail fork. Go straight on the left fork on the Oak Grove Trail. Switchback up the hillside, alternating between shady oak woodlands and exposed chaparral. At 0.7 miles, the path levels out on a 560-foot saddle by a signed junction with the Mount Manuel Trail. Bear right up the steps, leaving the oak canopy, and begin zigzagging up the

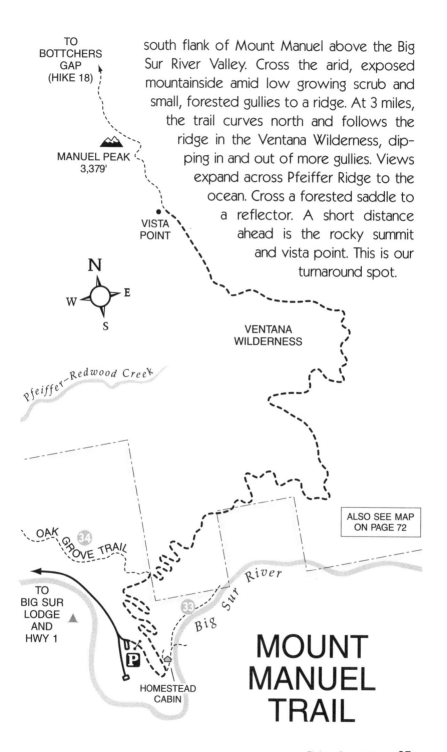

TO
BOTTCHERS
GAP
(HIKE 18)

MANUEL PEAK
3,379'

VISTA
POINT

N
W · E
S

VENTANA
WILDERNESS

Pfeiffer-Redwood Creek

OAK GROVE TRAIL

34

ALSO SEE MAP
ON PAGE 72

TO
BIG SUR
LODGE
AND
HWY 1

Big Sur River

33

P

HOMESTEAD
CABIN

south flank of Mount Manuel above the Big Sur River Valley. Cross the arid, exposed mountainside amid low growing scrub and small, forested gullies to a ridge. At 3 miles, the trail curves north and follows the ridge in the Ventana Wilderness, dipping in and out of more gullies. Views expand across Pfeiffer Ridge to the ocean. Cross a forested saddle to a reflector. A short distance ahead is the rocky summit and vista point. This is our turnaround spot.

MOUNT MANUEL TRAIL

Hike 36
Pine Ridge Trail to Terrace Creek
Pfeiffer Big Sur State Park

Hiking distance: 10.6 miles round trip
Hiking time: 5 hours
Elevation gain: 1,000 feet
Maps: U.S.G.S. Pfeiffer Point, Partington Ridge, Ventana Cross
Pfeiffer Big Sur State Park map

map next page

Summary of hike: The Pine Ridge Trail is a key access route to numerous camps and trails throughout the Ventana Wilderness. The most popular destination is the ten-mile overnight hike to the hot springs at Sykes Camp. This hike takes in the first 5.3 miles of the trail to Terrace Creek, traveling along the Big Sur River Valley 600—800 feet above the river. The hike may be combined with the Coast Ridge Trail (Hike 37) for a 12.5-mile loop.

Driving directions: The trail begins at the Big Sur Ranger Station, located 27 miles south of Carmel. Turn inland and drive 0.2 miles to the far end of the parking area at the trailhead.

Hiking directions: Take the signed trail at the far end of the parking lot into the shaded forest. Cross the hillside above the Big Sur River through tanbark oak and redwood groves, skirting the edge of the Big Sur Campground to an unsigned trail split. The left fork descends into the campground. Stay to the right and cross a water-carved ravine. Zigzag downhill and cross Post Creek. Climb out of the narrow canyon to vistas of the Big Sur Valley. Steadily gain elevation, traversing the cliffs above the Big Sur River Valley. The path alternates from exposed chaparral to shady draws. The Mount Manuel Trail is visible across the canyon. At 2.5 miles the trail enters the Ventana Wilderness by a boundary sign. Continue up the river valley to a junction with the trail to Ventana Camp at 4 miles. The left fork descends 1.2 miles to the camp, situated in a horseshoe bend of the Big Sur River. Continue east on the Pine Ridge Trail for 1.2

miles to Terrace Creek and a signed junction with the Terrace Creek Trail. Terrace Creek Camp sits above and to the right, straddling the creek in a beautiful grove of redwoods. This is the turnaround spot.

For the 12.5-mile loop, take the Terrace Creek Trail through the lush canyon for 1.6 miles to the Coast Ridge Road. Referencing the hiking directions below, follow the Coast Ridge Road west back to the parking area. Walk 1.7 miles on Highway 1 back to the Big Sur Ranger Station.

Hike 37
Coast Ridge Road to Terrace Creek Trail

Hiking distance: 8 miles round trip
Hiking time: 4 hours
Elevation gain: 1,600 feet
Maps: U.S.G.S. Pfeiffer Point and Partington Ridge

map
next page

Summary of hike: The Coast Ridge Road is a public right-of-way for hikers that is on a private, unpaved road. The road switchbacks to the top of the coastal ridge and follows the ridge for 30 miles. The trail offers spectacular views deep into the precipitous Ventana Wilderness, extending across the Big Sur Valley to the Pacific Ocean. This hike follows the first four miles to the Terrace Creek Trail. The hike may be combined with the Pine Ridge Trail (Hike 36) for a 12.5-mile loop.

Driving directions: From the Big Sur Ranger Station, located 27 miles south of Carmel, drive 1.7 miles south on Highway 1 to the signed Ventana Inn turnoff on the left. Turn left and drive 0.2 miles, staying to the right, to the signed Vista Point parking area on the right.

Hiking directions: Walk 0.1 mile up the paved road past Vista Point to the gated road on the right, where the paved road forks left. Pass the gate and take the unpaved Coast Ridge Road around Ventana Inn. The wooded road winds through the shaded oak, bay and redwood forest. At one mile, curve sharply left, crossing the trickling headwaters of Post Creek. Pass a narrow 30-foot waterfall cascading off a vertical rock wall on the right. Emerge from the forest, overlooking the redwood filled canyon, and steadily climb the open hillside trail with commanding coastal views. The winding road works slowly upward, following the mountain contours to the ridge and a hairpin right bend just before 2 miles. The serpentine road continues a steady but gentle uphill grade, crossing a saddle with views into the Ventana Wilderness. Cross several shady gullies and rolling grassy hills. At 4 miles, on a saddle just beyond a gated side road, is a signed junction with the Terrace Creek Trail on the left. This is our turnaround spot.

For a 12.5-mile loop, take the Terrace Creek Trail through the lush, wooded canyon. Continue 1.6 miles to Terrace Creek Camp in a redwood grove by a junction with the Pine Ridge Trail—Hike 36. Bear left and return via the Pine Ridge Trail (reference Hike 36). At the Big Sur Ranger Station, walk 1.7 miles southbound on Highway 1 back to the Ventana Inn turnoff.

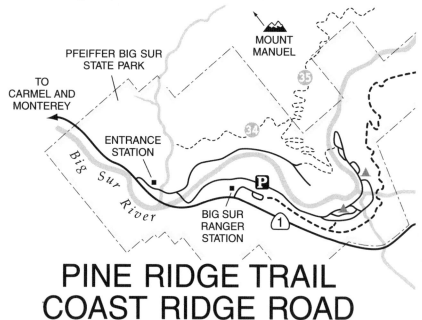

PINE RIDGE TRAIL
COAST RIDGE ROAD
HIKE 36 • HIKE 37

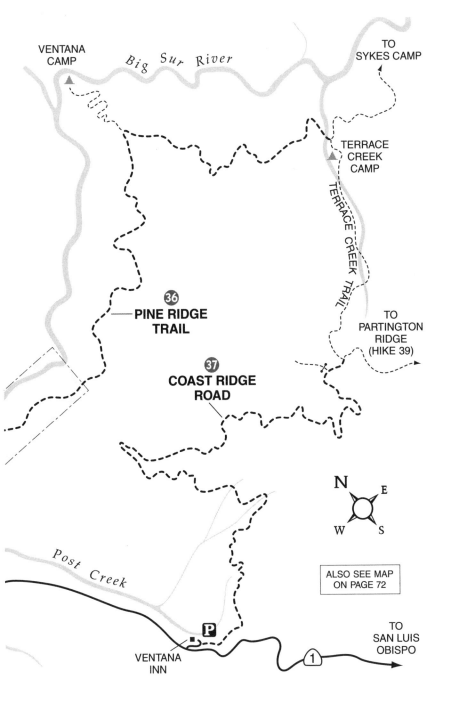

VENTANA CAMP

Big Sur River

TO SYKES CAMP

TERRACE CREEK CAMP

TERRACE CREEK TRAIL

36 **PINE RIDGE TRAIL**

37 **COAST RIDGE ROAD**

TO PARTINGTON RIDGE (HIKE 39)

N
E
W
S

ALSO SEE MAP ON PAGE 72

Post Creek

P

VENTANA INN

TO SAN LUIS OBISPO

1

Hike 38
Pfeiffer Beach

Hiking distance: 1 mile round trip
Hiking time: 30 minutes
Elevation gain: Level
Maps: U.S.G.S. Pfeiffer Point
Los Padres National Forest Northern Section Trail Map

Summary of hike: Pfeiffer Beach is a white sand beach surrounded by towering headland cliffs. Pfeiffer Point sits to the
south. Dramatic offshore sea stacks have been sculpted by the
wind and pounding surf, creating sea caves, eroded natural
arches and blowholes. On the beach, Sycamore Creek forms a
small lagoon as it empties into the Pacific. Pfeiffer Beach is part
of the Los Padres National Forest.

Driving directions: From the Big Sur Ranger Station, located
27 miles south of Carmel, drive 0.5 miles south on Highway 1 to
the unsigned Sycamore Canyon Road. Turn right and drive 2.2
miles down the narrow, winding road through Sycamore
Canyon to the parking lot. A parking fee is required.
From the signed Julia Pfeiffer Burns State Park entrance,
Sycamore Canyon Road is 9.8 miles north.

Hiking directions: From the west end of the parking area,
take the signed trail through a canopy of cypress trees to the
wide sandy beach. The beach is divided by Sycamore Creek,
which forms a small lagoon. Straight ahead are giant rock formations with natural arches and sea caves. A short distance to
the south are the steep cliffs of Pfeiffer Point. Beachcomb
along the shore from the point to the cliffs at the far north end
of the beach.

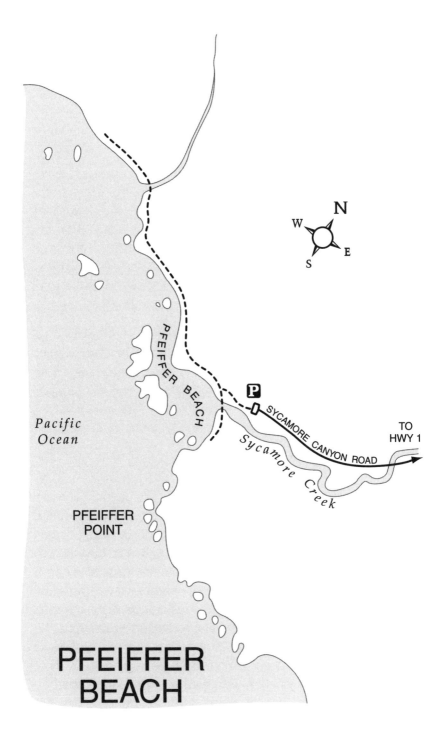

N

W E

S

PFEIFFER BEACH

Pacific
Ocean

P

SYCAMORE CANYON ROAD

TO
HWY 1

Sycamore Creek

PFEIFFER
POINT

PFEIFFER
BEACH

Hike 39
De Angulo Trail to Partington Ridge

Hiking distance: 5 miles round trip
Hiking time: 3 hours
Elevation gain: 1,500 feet
Maps: U.S.G.S. Partington Ridge

Summary of hike: The De Angulo Trail is a steep, unpaved, narrow road through the Wild Oak Ranch property. The serpentine road climbs up the mountain along the ocean side of Partington Ridge and leads to the Coast Ridge Trail at 3.8 miles. This hike heads up the first 2.5 miles to a knoll on Partington Ridge overlooking the Pacific Ocean and the interior mountains. Disregard the "No Trespassing" signs at the trailhead, as the road is a public right-of-way for hikers.

Driving directions: From the Big Sur Ranger Station, located 27 miles south of Carmel, drive 7.3 miles south on Highway 1 to parking pullouts on both sides of the highway by a gated road on the inland side of the highway. The gated road is 0.8 miles south of the large concrete Torre Canyon Bridge and 3 miles north of the signed Julia Pfeiffer Burns State Park entrance.

Hiking directions: Walk past the unsigned trail gate, and begin climbing steep switchbacks through a pine and eucalyptus forest. The narrow road quickly reaches beautiful coastal panoramas and passes a few isolated homes. At the top of the switchbacks, traverse the hillside to the north past a rolling grassy meadow. Continue through shady groves of bay and oak trees to a T-junction at 1.1 mile. The right fork leads to a home. Take the left fork, enjoying additional coastal views. Disregard the numerous side roads that lead to residences. Soon the road reaches a junction near a home in a redwood grove. Take the middle fork, straight ahead, following the trail sign. Switchbacks lead up to a ridge and curve right past a horse corral. A short distance ahead is a junction with the Partington Ridge Road by a ranch on the left. Straight ahead, the road begins a descent towards Partington Canyon. Bear sharply to the left and follow the fenceline, skirting the ranch to a grassy knoll on the left. After savoring the views, return along the same path.

To extend the hike, continue up the road a short distance to a signed junction. The left fork continues up Partington Ridge to the Coast Ridge Road (Hike 37).

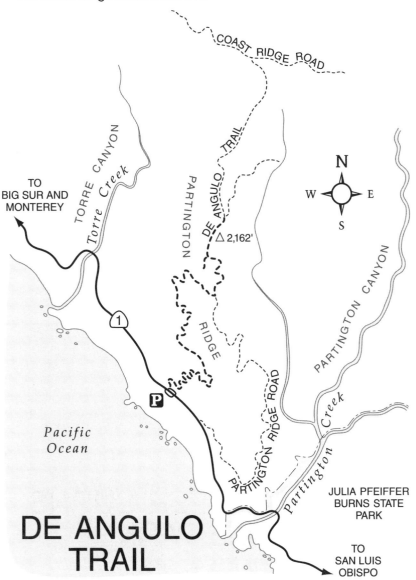

TO
BIG SUR AND
MONTEREY

N
W   E
S

TORRE CANYON

Torre Creek

PARTINGTON

DE ANGULO TRAIL

COAST RIDGE ROAD

△ 2,162'

PARTINGTON CANYON

Pacific
Ocean

P

RIDGE

1

PARTINGTON RIDGE ROAD

Partington Creek

Partington Creek

JULIA PFEIFFER
BURNS STATE
PARK

DE ANGULO
TRAIL

TO
SAN LUIS
OBISPO

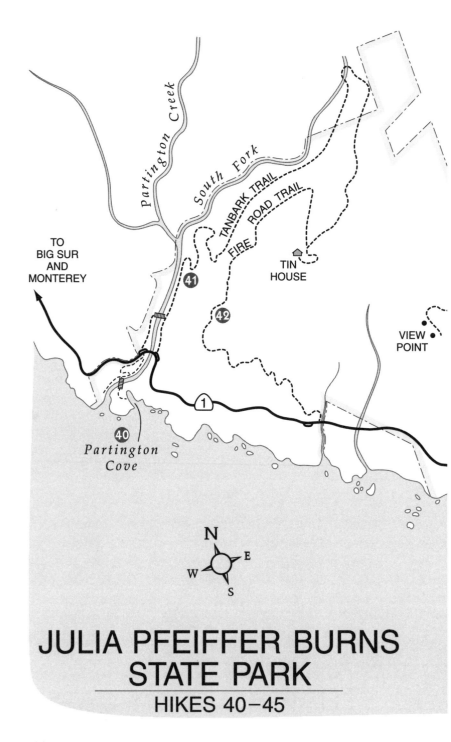

JULIA PFEIFFER BURNS
STATE PARK
HIKES 40–45

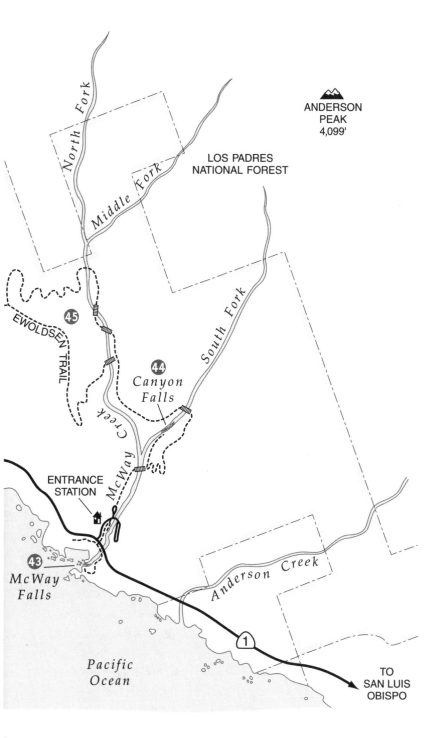

ANDERSON
PEAK
4,099'

North Fork

Middle Fork

LOS PADRES
NATIONAL FOREST

South Fork

EWOLDSEN TRAIL

45

44
Canyon
Falls

McWay Creek

ENTRANCE
STATION

43
McWay
Falls

Anderson Creek

1

Pacific
Ocean

TO
SAN LUIS
OBISPO

Hike 40
Partington Cove
Julia Pfeiffer Burns State Park

Hiking distance: 1 mile round trip
Hiking time: 1 hour
Elevation gain: 280 feet
Maps: U.S.G.S. Partington Ridge
Julia Pfeiffer Burns State Park map

Summary of hike: Partington Cove sits at the northern boundary of Julia Pfeiffer Burns State Park. The trail to the cove descends down Partington Canyon on an old dirt road. Partington Creek, which carved the canyon, empties into the ocean at the small rocky west cove. A 120-foot tunnel has been cut through the cliffs, leading to the east cove and Partington Landing. The landing was used as a shipping dock for timber in the 1880s by homesteader John Partington.

Driving directions: From the Big Sur Ranger Station, located 27 miles south of Carmel, drive 8.5 miles south on Highway 1 to the wide parking pullouts on both sides of the highway by Partington Bridge, where the road curves across Partington Creek and the canyon. The pullouts are 1.9 miles north of the signed Julia Pfeiffer Burns State Park entrance.

Hiking directions: Head west on the ocean side of Highway 1 past the trailhead gate. Descend on the eroded granite road along the north canyon wall, high above Partington Creek. The old road weaves downhill to the creek and a junction with an interpretive sign. The left fork follows Partington Creek upstream under a dense forest canopy. Take the right fork 50 yards to a second junction. The left route crosses a wooden footbridge over Partington Creek and leads to the tunnel carved through the granite wall. The tunnel ends on the east cove, where remnants of Partington Landing remain. Return to the junction by the bridge, and take the path that is now on your left. Follow the north bank of Partington Creek to an enclosed beach cove surrounded by the steep cliffs of Partington Point. Return along the same trail.

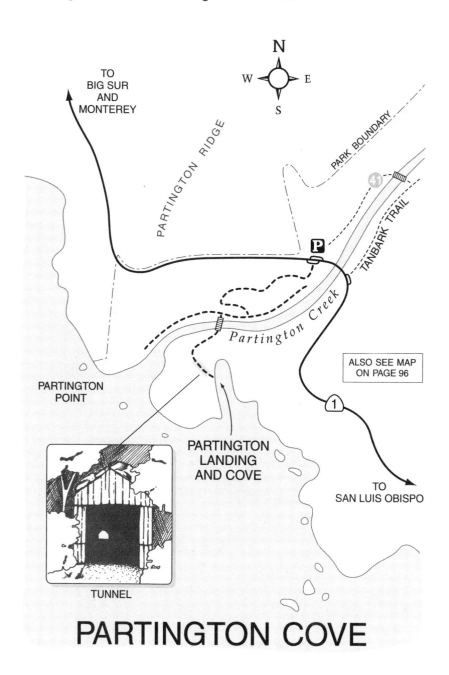

N

W —⇪— E

S

TO
BIG SUR
AND
MONTEREY

PARTINGTON RIDGE

PARK BOUNDARY

41

P

TANBARK TRAIL

Partington Creek

ALSO SEE MAP
ON PAGE 96

1

PARTINGTON
POINT

PARTINGTON
LANDING
AND COVE

TO
SAN LUIS OBISPO

TUNNEL

PARTINGTON COVE

Hike 41
Tanbark Trail to Tin House
Julia Pfeiffer Burns State Park

Hiking distance: 6.4 miles round trip
Hiking time: 4 hours
Elevation gain: 1,900 feet
Maps: U.S.G.S. Partington Ridge
Julia Pfeiffer Burns State Park map

map
next page

Summary of hike: The Tanbark Trail climbs up Partington Canyon to a grassy meadow with spectacular coastal views at the abandoned Tin House. The path parallels Partington Creek through a dense forest of huge redwoods, tanbark oaks and a lush understory of ferns. Switchbacks lead up the canyon wall to the ridge separating Partington and McWay Canyons. The hike can be combined with the Fire Road Trail (Hike 42) for a 6.4-mile loop.

Driving directions: From the Big Sur Ranger Station, located 27 miles south of Carmel, drive 8.5 miles south on Highway 1 to the wide parking pullouts on both sides of the highway by Partington Bridge, where the road curves across Partington Creek and the canyon. The pullouts are 1.9 miles north of the signed Julia Pfeiffer Burns State Park entrance.

Hiking directions: From the inland side of the road, take the path leading into the steep walled canyon from either side of the bridge. Both trails join together by a wooden footbridge crossing over Partington Creek. The Tanbark Trail continues upstream on the east side of the creek, passing huge rock formations, redwood groves, pools, cascades, waterfalls, ferns and mossy boulders. Cross a tributary stream by McLaughlin Grove, and head up the canyon wall on a few switchbacks, leaving the creek and canyon floor. Weave up the mountain to a sharp left switchback. A short detour to the right leads to a ridge overlooking Partington Point. Return to the trail and traverse the canyon wall through tanbark oaks and redwoods.

Cross planks over the South Fork of Partington Creek. Sharply switchback to the right, and recross the creek by a bench in a redwood grove. Continue uphill to the south, reaching the high point of the hike at a trail sign. Descend to a T-junction with the Fire Road Trail (Hike 42). Bear left on the unpaved road, and descend a short distance, curving to the right to the abandoned Tin House. Below the house is a grassy meadow with inspiring views of the Big Sur Coast. Return along the same trail, or combine this hike with the Fire Road Trail for a 6.4-mile loop, returning 0.9 miles on Highway 1 to the trailhead.

Hike 42
Fire Road Trail to Tin House
Julia Pfeiffer Burns State Park

Hiking distance: 4.6 miles round trip

Hiking time: 2.5 hours

Elevation gain: 1,600 feet

Maps: U.S.G.S. Partington Ridge
 Julia Pfeiffer Burns State Park map

map
next page

Summary of hike: The Fire Road Trail resembles more of a trail than a road. The road begins on the coastal cliffs and heads inland, weaving in and out of gullies to Partington Canyon. The wide trail contours the east wall of the canyon, rich with coastal redwoods, tanbark oaks and shade-loving plants. The trail ends at the Tin House, a boarded up tin building on the ridge separating Partington and McWay Canyons. Below the building is a grassy meadow with great coastal vistas from an elevation of 1,950 feet. The trail can be combined with the Tanbark Trail (Hike 41) for a 6.4-mile loop.

Driving directions: From the Big Sur Ranger Station, located 27 miles south of Carmel, drive 9.3 miles south on Highway 1 to the signed Vista Point parking pullout on the right. The pullout is 1.1 mile north of the signed Julia Pfeiffer Burns State Park entrance.

Hiking directions: Head 75 yards southbound on Highway 1 to the gated Fire Road on the inland side of the highway. Walk around the trail gate into a shady redwood grove, paralleling a trickling stream on the right. Curve left, emerging from the trees, and climb to an overlook of the coast and offshore rocks. The trail follows the coastal cliffs along the oceanfront mountains. As you near Partington Canyon, a thousand feet above Partington Cove, the trail curves right and enters the canyon. The views extend across the canyon to homes on the south-facing cliffs. Curve along the contours of the mountain, winding uphill on the serpentine path through redwoods and tanbark oaks. A few switchbacks aid in the climb through the shady forest. The road tops out at a signed junction with the Tanbark Trail (Hike 41) on the left. Continue straight ahead, gently descending for a short distance and looping to the right. The trail ends at the abandoned Tin House and the grassy meadow overlook. Return along the same trail, or combine this hike with the Tanbark Trail for a 6.4-mile loop, returning 0.9 miles on Highway 1 to the Vista Point pullouts.

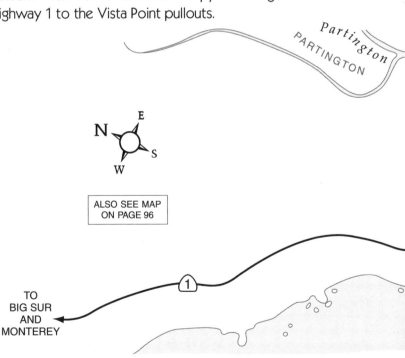

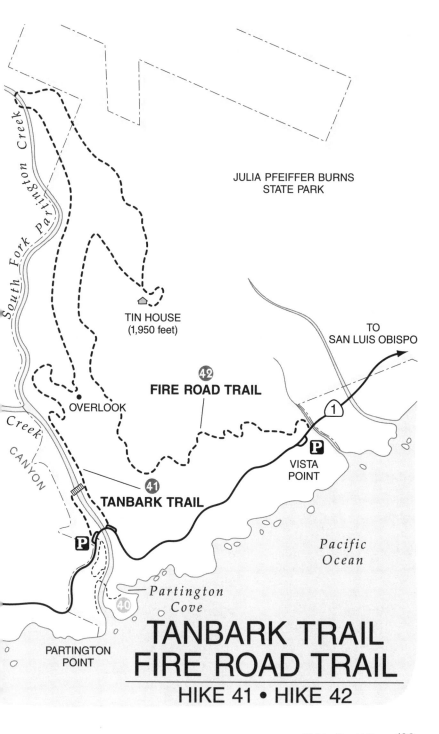

JULIA PFEIFFER BURNS
STATE PARK

South Fork Partington Creek

TIN HOUSE
(1,950 feet)

TO
SAN LUIS OBISPO

42
FIRE ROAD TRAIL

OVERLOOK

Creek

CANYON

1

P
VISTA
POINT

41
TANBARK TRAIL

P

Pacific
Ocean

Partington
Cove

40

PARTINGTON
POINT

TANBARK TRAIL
FIRE ROAD TRAIL
HIKE 41 • HIKE 42

Hike 43
McWay Falls and Saddle Rock
Julia Pfeiffer Burns State Park

Hiking distance: 0.7 miles round trip
Hiking time: 30 minutes
Elevation gain: 50 feet
Maps: U.S.G.S. Partington Ridge
      Julia Pfeiffer Burns State Park map

Summary of hike: McWay Falls pours 80 feet onto the sand along the edge of the Pacific at the mouth of McWay Canyon. The waterfall drops off the granite bluff in a scenic, wooded beach cove lined with offshore rocks. The Waterfall Overlook Trail, a handicap accessible trail, leads to a viewing area of McWay Cove and the cataract on the 100-foot high bluffs (cover photo). The pristine beach itself is not accessible. On the south side of the bay is a scenic overlook at a cypress-shaded picnic area and environmental camp adjacent to Saddle Rock.

Driving directions: From the Big Sur Ranger Station, located 27 miles south of Carmel, drive 10.4 miles south on Highway 1 to the signed Julia Pfeiffer Burns State Park. Turn left (inland) and park in the day-use parking lot.

Hiking directions: Descend the steps across the road from the restrooms. At the base of the steps, bear right and head southwest on the signed Waterfall Trail. Follow the north canyon wall above the creek, and walk through the tunnel under Highway 1 to a T-junction. The left fork leads to the Saddle Rock Overlook. For now, take the right fork along the cliffs. Cross a wooden footbridge with great views of McWay Falls pouring onto the sand. Beyond the bridge is an observation deck with expansive coastal views. After enjoying the sights, return to the junction, and take the footpath towards the south end of the bay. Walk through a canopy of old-growth eucalyptus trees high above the falls. Descend to the trail's end at a 206-foot overlook in a cypress grove by the camping and picnic area.

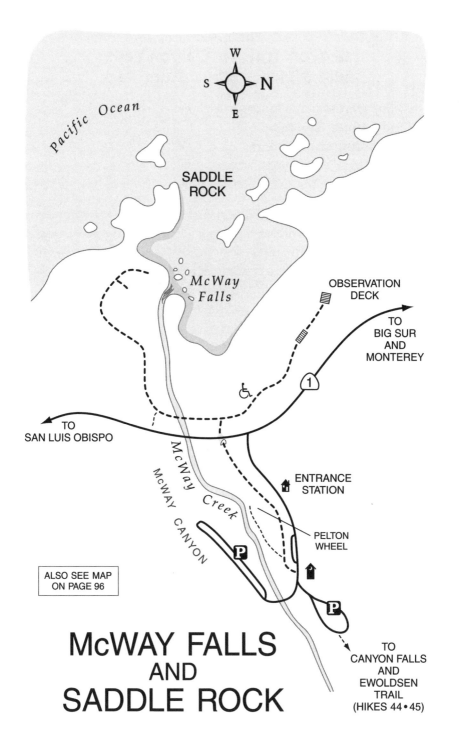

Pacific Ocean

SADDLE ROCK

McWay Falls

OBSERVATION DECK

TO BIG SUR AND MONTEREY

1

TO SAN LUIS OBISPO

McWay Creek

McWay CANYON

ENTRANCE STATION

PELTON WHEEL

ALSO SEE MAP ON PAGE 96

P

P

TO CANYON FALLS AND EWOLDSEN TRAIL (HIKES 44 • 45)

McWAY FALLS
AND
SADDLE ROCK

Hike 44
Canyon Trail to Canyon Falls
Julia Pfeiffer Burns State Park

Hiking distance: 0.7 miles round trip
Hiking time: 30 minutes
Elevation gain: 200 feet
Maps: U.S.G.S. Partington Ridge
      Julia Pfeiffer Burns State Park map

Summary of hike: The Canyon Trail begins on the Ewoldsen Trail (Hike 45) and meanders through a rich, coastal redwood forest. The shaded path parallels McWay Creek up the canyon and ends at Canyon Falls, a long, narrow, two-tiered waterfall on the South Fork of McWay Creek. The 70-foot cataract cascades off fern covered rock cliffs in a lush grotto at the back of the serene canyon.

Driving directions: From the Big Sur Ranger Station, located 27 miles south of Carmel, drive 10.4 miles south on Highway 1 to the signed Julia Pfeiffer Burns State Park. Turn left (inland) and park in the day-use parking lot.

Hiking directions: Take the signed Canyon and Ewoldsen Trails from the upper end of the parking lot. Follow the watercourse of McWay Creek upstream past the picnic area shaded by redwoods. Continue along the west bank of the creek through the dense coastal redwood forest and communities of ferns and redwood sorrel. Cross a wooden footbridge over the creek to the east bank, just below the confluence of the South Fork and Main Fork of McWay Creek. A short distance upstream is a posted junction. The right fork climbs the canyon wall on the Ewoldsen Trail (Hike 45). Take the left fork, staying close to the creek on the Canyon Trail. The narrow, cliffside path ends at the base of the waterfall. Return along the same path.

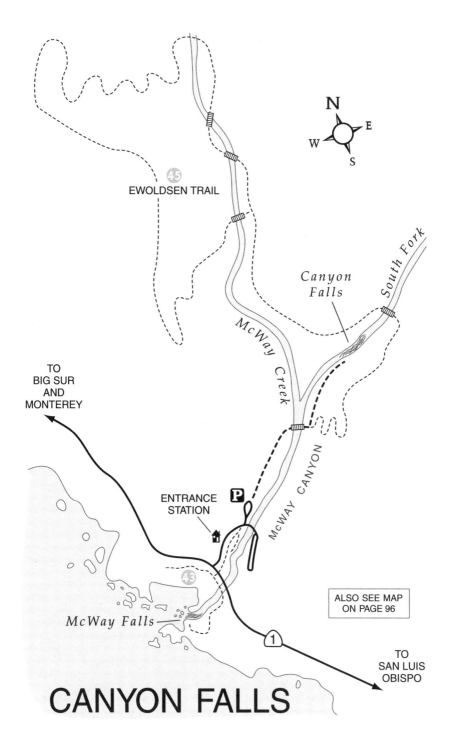

EWOLDSEN TRAIL

N
E
W
S

South Fork

Canyon Falls

McWay Creek

TO
BIG SUR
AND
MONTEREY

McWAY CANYON

ENTRANCE
STATION

P

ALSO SEE MAP
ON PAGE 96

McWay Falls

1

TO
SAN LUIS
OBISPO

CANYON FALLS

Hike 45
Ewoldsen Trail
Julia Pfeiffer Burns State Park

Hiking distance: 4.5 mile loop
Hiking time: 2.5 hours
Elevation gain: 1,600 feet
Maps: U.S.G.S. Partington Ridge
Julia Pfeiffer Burns State Park map

Summary of hike: The Ewoldsen Trail follows McWay Creek through a dense coastal redwood forest in McWay Canyon. The trail crosses several bridges as it heads up to the ridge separating McWay and Partington Canyons. From the grassy coastal cliffs are amazing overlooks perched on the edge of the cliffs. The views extend from the north to the south, showcasing the jagged coastline and endless mountain ridges and valleys.

Driving directions: From the Big Sur Ranger Station, located 27 miles south of Carmel, drive 10.4 miles south on Highway 1 to the signed Julia Pfeiffer Burns State Park. Turn left (inland) and park in the day-use parking lot.

Hiking directions: From the upper end of the parking area, take the signed Ewoldsen Trail into a dark redwood forest. Follow McWay Creek past the picnic area, and cross the footbridge over the creek. Continue upstream past the confluence of the South Fork and Main Fork of McWay Creek to a posted junction. The left fork leads to Canyon Falls (Hike 44). Take the Ewoldsen Trail up the switchback to the right, leaving the canyon floor and creek. Zigzag up the south wall of the canyon, and cross a wooden footbridge over the South Fork. Traverse the hillside up the mountain contours, rejoining the Main Fork of McWay Creek, where views extend down canyon to the sea. Follow the watercourse above the creek to a signed junction at one mile, beginning the loop. Take the right fork along the east bank of the creek. Cross two bridges over the creek, passing cascades, small waterfalls, pools, outcroppings and moss covered boulders. Cross a log bridge over the creek, and ascend the west canyon wall. Enter an oak woodland and follow the hillside path to a signed junction. Detour to the right a quarter mile to the viewpoint on the 1,800-foot oceanfront cliffs. Take a break and enjoy the vistas. Return to the junction and continue on the loop. The winding path descends along the oceanfront cliffs, then curves left into the forested canyon. Complete the loop at the bridge over McWay Creek, and return to the right.

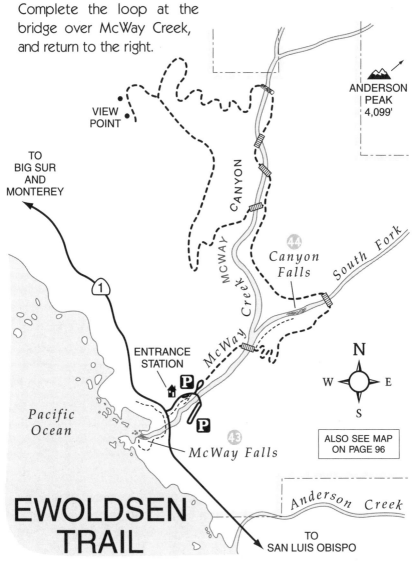

Hike 46
Waterfall—Mesa Loop
Garland Ranch Regional Park

Hiking distance: 3.5 mile loop
Hiking time: 1.5 hours
Elevation gain: 600 feet
Maps: U.S.G.S. Seaside and Mt. Carmel
       Garland Ranch Regional Park map

Summary of hike: Garland Ranch Regional Park lies along the Santa Lucia Mountains adjacent to the Carmel River. A network of hiking trails runs throughout the park. This loop hike visits Garland Ranch Falls, a 70-foot cataract that falls from a sandstone cliff in an enclosed fern-filled canyon. The hike is enjoyable year-round, but to experience the cascade of the ephemeral waterfall, plan your hike after a rain. Beyond the falls, the forested trail continues to La Mesa, a flat river terrace and wildlife habitat pond above the valley floor.

Driving directions: From Highway 1 in Carmel, take Carmel Valley Road, and drive 8.6 miles east to the Garland Ranch Regional Park parking lot on the right.

Hiking directions: Follow the gravel path to the right. Bear left at the bridge, crossing over the Carmel River to a trail junction. Bear left, passing the visitor center on the Lupine Loop. Walk southeast through the meadow to a posted junction. Go to the left on the Waterfall Trail, following the rocky riverbed. Ascend the hillside and enter the tree-shaded slopes, passing the Cliff Trail on the right. Traverse the cliffside up the gulch, and cross a wooden footbridge into the steep-walled box canyon at the base of the transient waterfall. Climb steps and cross another footbridge, leaving the canyon and emerging into an oak woodland with a lush understory of ferns and moss. Pass through a trail gate to a junction with the Vaquero Trail on the left. Continue straight ahead, steadily gaining elevation to a large grassy mesa with benches and a 4-way junction at 1.6

miles. The right fork, the Mesa Trail, is the return route. First, continue 125 yards to La Mesa Pond. After the pond, return to the junction, and take the Mesa Trail to the north. The trail gently winds down the hillside, passing junctions with the Sky, Hawk and Fern Trails. Cross a trickling stream in the fern filled drainage to a T-junction with the Lupine Loop above the meadow. Bear right, drop into the meadow and complete the loop.

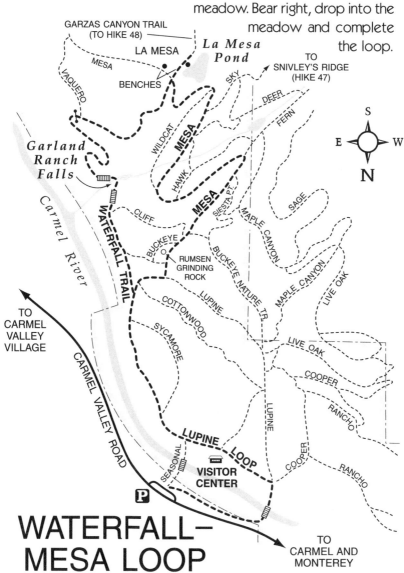

WATERFALL–
MESA LOOP

Hike 47
Snivley's Ridge—Sky Loop
Garland Ranch Regional Park

Hiking distance: 6 mile loop
Hiking time: 3 hours
Elevation gain: 1,600 feet
Maps: U.S.G.S. Seaside and Mt. Carmel
Garland Ranch Regional Park map

Summary of hike: Garland Park stretches from the willow-lined Carmel River to the crest of the Santa Lucia Range. This hike begins at the river and climbs through oak woodlands to Snivley's Ridge at the mountain crest, 1,600 feet above Carmel Valley. From the ridge are sweeping, unobstructed birds-eye views of Carmel Valley, the Monterey Peninsula, Salinas and the interior Santa Lucia Mountains. Portions of the Snivley's Ridge Trail are tirelessly steep and require frequent rest stops.

Driving directions: From Highway 1 in Carmel, take Carmel Valley Road, and drive 8.6 miles east to the Garland Ranch Regional Park parking lot on the right.

Hiking directions: Take the path to the right, and cross the bridge over the Carmel River to a signed trail split. Bear left, passing the visitor center on the Lupine Loop. Follow the meadow to a junction with the Waterfall Trail (Hike 46). Stay on the Lupine Loop, pass the Cottonwood Trail and climb a small rise to a bluff above the meadow. At the signed junction, bear left on the Mesa Trail. Head up the lush drainage and cross a trickling stream. The winding path passes Buckeye, Siesta Point, Fern, Hawk and Sky Trails, all on the right. At Sky Trail, begin the loop to the left, staying on the Mesa Trail. Emerge onto La Mesa, a huge grassy terrace at a 4-way junction. Take the Garzas Canyon Trail on the right. Pass La Mesa Pond, a wildlife habitat pond, and continue into the shady grove of stately oaks at the base of the mountain. Curve left and climb the mountain slope to the ridge at a junction with Snivley's Ridge Trail. Begin a very steep ascent to the right on Snivley's Ridge. Climb through oak groves and small meadows on the east-facing cliffs above Garzas Canyon. The eroded path mercifully levels out at a fenceline by Snivley's Corral, a sitting bench and trail junction. After resting, descend on the winding Sky Trail to an elevated perch overlooking La Mesa Pond and the network of trails. Stay to the right past the Sage and Deer Trails, completing the loop at the Mesa Trail. Bear left on the Mesa Trail, retracing your steps back to the trailhead.

Garzas Cr.

48

GARZAS
CANYON
TRAIL

OAKVIEW

SNIVLEY'S RIDGE TRAIL

SNIVLEY'S
CORRAL

BENCH

PINYON PEAK
2,249'

GARZAS CANYON TR

VALLEY
VISTA

LA MESA

BENCH

La Mesa
Pond

SKY TRAIL

VAQUERO

MESA

DEER

FERN

SAGE

WILDCAT

MESA

HAWK

46

SAGE

CLIFF

MESA

SIESTA

WATERFALL

BUCKEYE

BUCKEYE

RUMSEN
GRINDING
ROCK

MAPLE CAN

MAPLE CAN

SAGE

S

E ⊕ W

N

TO
CARMEL
VALLEY
VILLAGE

LUPINE

SYCAMORE

LIVE OAK

CARMEL VALLEY ROAD

LUPINE LOOP

VISITOR
CENTER

LUPINE

COOPER

SEASONAL
BRIDGE

P

TO
CARMEL AND
MONTEREY

SNIVLEY'S
RIDGE–SKY
LOOP

Hike 48
Garzas Canyon—Redwood Canyon— Terrace Loop
Garland Ranch Regional Park

Hiking distance: 3.6 mile loop
Hiking time: 2 hours
Elevation gain: 800 feet
Maps: U.S.G.S. Seaside and Mt. Carmel
     Garland Ranch Regional Park map

map
next page

Summary of hike: Garzas Canyon is a stream-fed canyon bisecting Garland Ranch. The Garzas Canyon Trail heads up the lush garden-like canyon past rock-lined pools and numerous creek crossings. The hike ends in Redwood Canyon, a remote side canyon with clusters of towering redwoods.

Driving directions: From Highway 1 in Carmel, take Carmel Valley Road, and drive 10.3 miles east to Boronda Road on the right. The turnoff is 1.7 miles past the signed Garland Ranch parking lot. Turn right and drive 0.6 miles, crossing over the Carmel River to the end of the road. Turn left on East Garzas Road, and continue 0.2 miles to the signed trail on the right. Park alongside the road. A signed connector trail into Garzas Canyon begins a quarter mile ahead at the end of the road.

Hiking directions: Hike into the shady oak grove, passing the River Trail. Head up the forested slope past the Veeder Trail on the left (Hike 49) to the signed junction with the Terrace Trail, our return route. Begin the loop to the right on the Garzas Canyon Trail. Switchbacks descend to Garzas Creek at the canyon floor. Head up canyon and cross a long wooden footbridge over the creek. The path climbs numerous small rises, then dips back to the floor and a junction. The Garzas Canyon Trail leads up the canyon wall to La Mesa. Stay to the left on the creekside path. Cross another footbridge over the creek to a junction with the East Ridge Trail. (For a shorter hike, the East Ridge Trail connects with the Terrace Trail.) Go to the right and pass through a trail gate on the Redwood Canyon Trail. Continue up canyon, crossing the creek four more times. At the fourth crossing, leave Garzas Creek, and head up Redwood Canyon. Pass clusters of large redwoods in the narrow side canyon. A half mile up the canyon, a bridge crosses the stream at a junction. This is the return route. First, continue up Redwood Canyon through the forest, rich with ferns and magnificent redwoods. The canyon splits in a wide flat area covered with redwoods. The trail follows the right canyon and soon fades away. Return to the bridge and cross, heading up the east canyon wall. Pass through a trail gate to a Y-junction with the East Ridge Trail. Take the left fork fifty yards to a signed junction. Bear right on the Terrace Trail. Traverse the narrow cliffside path above Garzas Canyon, following the contours of the mountain. Climb the steps and complete the loop at the Garzas Canyon Trail. Return to the right.

Hike 49
Veeder—East Ridge—Terrace Loop
Garland Ranch Regional Park

Hiking distance: 3.5 mile loop
Hiking time: 2 hours
Elevation gain: 1,300 feet
Maps: U.S.G.S. Carmel Valley, Mt. Carmel and Seaside
      Garland Ranch Regional Park map

**map
next page**

Summary of hike: This loop hike climbs hundreds of feet to an overlook in a mountain meadow. The panoramic views include Garzas Canyon, Redwood Canyon, Snivley's Ridge, Carmel Valley and the ocean at Monterey Bay. The trail winds through oak woodlands and traverses a narrow, cliffside path above Garzas Canyon.

Driving directions: Same as Hike 48.

Hiking directions: Take the signed Garzas Trail through the oak woodland. Cross the River Trail and head up the slope to a signed junction on the left. Bear left on the Veeder Trail, and wind up the oak-studded hill past ferns and poison oak. Steadily climb the east-facing hillside overlooking Carmel Valley. Curve right up the side canyon to a bench in a clearing with views of Garzas Canyon and Snivley's Ridge. Beyond the bench, climb to a ridge, passing through a trail gate to a saddle and a signed junction with the East Ridge Trail. The left branch climbs up to Vasquez Knob. Before taking the right fork (the return route), descend into the open meadow to a bench at a vernal pool. Return to the junction and ascend the small hill to a knoll, the highest point on this hike. The 360-degree vistas extend to the sea at Monterey Bay. Descend to the west, overlooking Redwood Canyon and the towering trees.

The path quickly drops down the north wall of Redwood Canyon to a junction. The left fork leads up Redwood Canyon (Hike 48). Take the right fork 50 yards to a junction with the Terrace Trail on the right. Head right, traversing the cliffs on the narrow path above the canyon. Weave in and out of ravines along the contours of the canyon. Climb some steps to a junction with the Garzas Canyon Trail. Bear to the right, completing the loop at the Veeder Trail. Return on the same route.

VASQUEZ

SPRING

GABILAN

50

LAURELES

RIVER TR.

W

S

E

N

DE LOS HELECHOS ROAD

ESQUILINE ROAD

PASO HONDO RD

Carmel Valley Village

HIKE 48
GARZAS–REDWOOD CANYONS LOOP

HIKE 49
VEEDER–EAST RIDGE LOOP

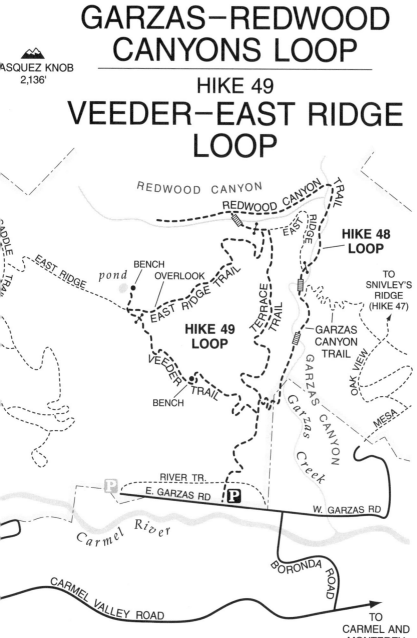

Hike 50
Laureles—Vasquez—Spring Loop
Garland Ranch Regional Park

Hiking distance: 5.5 miles round trip
Hiking time: 3 hours
Elevation gain: 1,700 feet
Maps: U.S.G.S. Carmel Valley and Mt. Carmel
Garland Ranch Regional Park map

Summary of hike: This loop hike lies at the southeast end, and lightly hiked area, of Garland Ranch. The trail steeply ascends the mountain to Vasquez Ridge at an overlook with a bench. The path follows the ridge, overlooking Hitchcock Canyon and Carmel Valley, then returns through an oak-filled and spring-fed canyon beneath the ridge.

Driving directions: From Highway 1 in Carmel, take Carmel Valley Road, and drive 11.9 miles east to Esquiline Road on the right. The turnoff is just past Carmel Valley Village. Turn right and drive 0.2 miles, crossing Rosie's Bridge over the Carmel River, to De Los Helechos Road. Turn right and park at the end of the street.

Hiking directions: From the end of De Los Helechos Road, walk through the Lazy Oaks right-of-way past a few homes to the Garland Park entrance. Follow the path through oak groves to a posted trail split. Curve left, quickly reaching a second junction. The right fork follows the River Trail. Curve left on the Laureles Trail, and ascend the forested hillside. Climb through the oak woodland to magnificent valley views. Continue climbing through the forest, emerging on the grassy ridge at 1.3 miles. On the ridge is a bench, a junction and magnificent views. A detour left leads 0.2 miles through oak-dotted meadows to the fenced park boundary. Return to the junction and take the Vasquez Trail 40 yards to a posted trail fork. Begin the loop to the left, staying on the Vasquez Trail. Follow the ridge up the meadow along the south boundary, overlooking Hitchcock Canyon. At the Y-junction, another short detour left leads to the hilltop summit at the park boundary. The right fork heads downhill on the Saddle Trail, crossing the head of Redwood Canyon. Pass a junction on the left with the East Ridge Trail (Hike 49), and skirt around the left side of the knoll. Steadily descend to a Y-fork. Take the Spring Trail to the right, and head downhill into the oak-filled canyon beneath Vasquez Ridge. Pass the narrow Gabilan Trail on the left to a trough, spring and water tank on the canyon floor. Curve left down canyon, and ascend the hillside, completing the loop on the ridge. Return on the Laureles Trail.

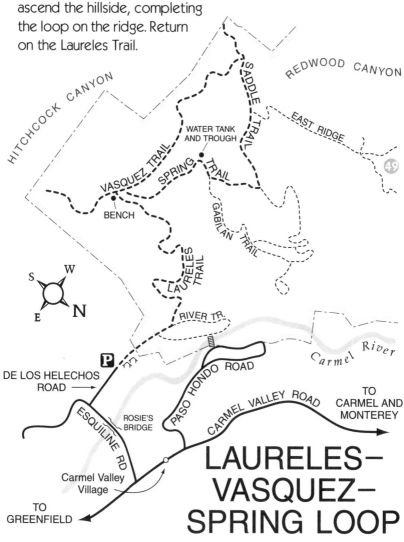

Hike 51
Carmel River Trail to Danish Creek
Los Padres Reservoir

Hiking distance: 5.6 miles round trip
Hiking time: 2.5 hours
Elevation gain: 300 feet
Maps: U.S.G.S. Carmel Valley and Ventana Cones
        Los Padres National Forest Northern Section Trail Map

map next page

Summary of hike: The Los Padres Reservoir is nestled in a gorgeous valley surrounded by the forested mountains. This hike follows the long reservoir from one end to the other. The forested path contours the mountains along the western slope of the reservoir. Be cautious of ticks along the trail during the winter season.

Driving directions: From Highway 1 in Carmel, take Carmel Valley Road and drive 16 miles east to the signed Los Padres Dam/Cachagua Road turnoff. Turn right and drive 5.8 miles on the winding road to the posted Nason Road turnoff in the community of Cachagua. Turn right and continue 0.6 miles to the large parking area at the end of the public road.

Hiking directions: Walk through the trailhead gate. Follow the unpaved dam road (Carmel River Trail) up the Carmel River Canyon. Pass stately, twisted oaks to a large open flat with several forking side roads. Stay on the main road to the dam spillway in a granite gorge at a half mile. Cross the gorge on the bridge, and head up the road past the waterfall. Curve right to the Los Padres Dam and overlook of the reservoir. Walk toward the hills on the west side of the reservoir. Curve sharply south (left) and traverse the hillside above the lake, enjoying a birds-eye view of the lake and surrounding mountains. Several side paths on the left descend to the reservoir. The wide trail narrows to a single track and reaches a signed junction at 1.7 miles. The Carmel River Trail continues straight along the west side of the reservoir. The right fork is the Big Pines Trail (Hike 52).

Stay on the Carmel River Trail parallel to the reservoir. The trail alternates from shady forest to open chaparral as it follows the contours of the mountain on the cliff's narrow edge. Near the south end of the lake is an overlook of the snake-shaped reservoir. Gradually descend with the aid of switchbacks to Danish Creek. Follow the creek upstream to a rocky beach at 2.8 miles, our turnaround spot.

To continue, ford the creek and follow the Carmel River Canyon, reaching Bluff Camp at 4 miles.

Hike 52
Big Pine Trail to Danish Creek Camp
Los Padres Reservoir

Hiking distance: 7 miles round trip
Hiking time: 3.5 hours
Elevation gain: 1,300 feet
Maps: U.S.G.S. Carmel Valley
       Los Padres National Forest Northern Section Trail Map

map
next page

Summary of hike: The Big Pine Trail lies on the west side of the Los Padres Reservoir in a scenic mountain valley. Hikes 51 and 52 begin on the Carmel River Trail, curving around the dam and spillway along the western slope of the reservoir. The Big Pine Trail—this hike—switchbacks up to a ridge that overlooks the reservoir and surrounding wilderness area. A short spur trail drops into a small canyon at Danish Camp near the confluence of Danish and Rattlesnake Creeks. Watch for ticks, which are prevalent during the wet season.

Driving directions: From Highway 1 in Carmel, take Carmel Valley Road and drive 16 miles east to the signed Los Padres Dam/Cachagua Road turnoff. Turn right and drive 5.8 miles on the winding road to the posted Nason Road turnoff in the community of Cachagua. Turn right and continue 0.6 miles to the large parking area at the end of the public road.

Hiking directions: Follow the directions for Hike 51 to the signed junction at 1.7 miles (noted on map). Bear right on the Big Pines Trail up the narrow hillside path. Weave up the side canyon, steadily climbing to elevated views of the lake. The trail levels out on a saddle at the head of the canyon. Panoramic views extend west to Blue Rock Ridge, east to Hennicksons Ridge, and south to Elephant Mountain and Uncle Sam Mountain. Follow the ridge to a posted trail split at the high point of the hike (2,058 feet). Leave the Big Pines Trail, and bear left on the Danish Creek Trail. Zigzag down the steep hillside 0.7 miles to Danish Creek Camp. The camp is next to Danish Creek on an open flat with a large live oak. Explore the trail along Danish Creek. Rattlesnake Creek is a short distance upstream. Return along the same trail.

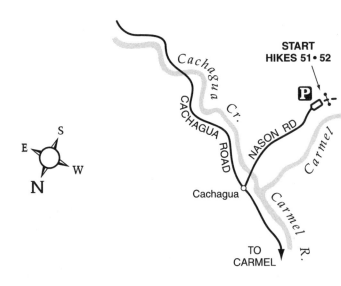

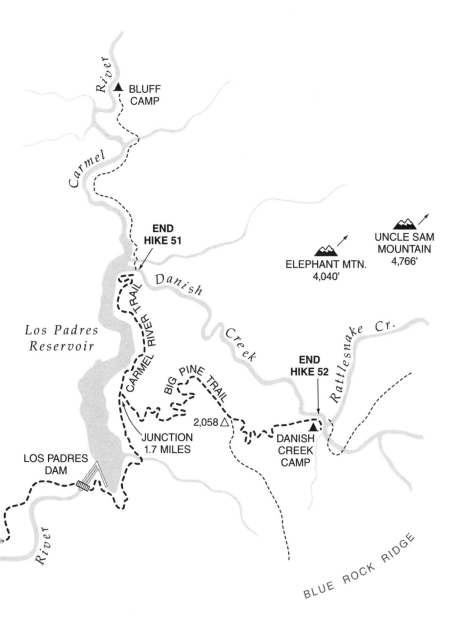

LOS PADRES RESERVOIR
CARMEL RIVER TRAIL • BIG PINE TRAIL
HIKE 51 • HIKE 52

Hike 53
Anastasia Trail to Cahoon Spring

Hiking distance: 4.8 miles round trip
Hiking time: 2.5 hours
Elevation gain: 900 feet
Maps: U.S.G.S. Chews Ridge
         Ventana Wilderness Map

Summary of hike: Cahoon Spring is a natural spring located in Bear Trap Canyon. The spring flows from a pipe in a glen shaded by towering black oaks. The lightly traveled hiking and equestrian trail accesses Bear Trap Canyon through a lush forest from Anastasia Canyon along the Anastasia Trail.

Driving directions: From Highway 1 in Carmel, take Carmel Valley Road and drive 23 miles southeast (passing through Carmel Valley Village at 11.5 miles) to Tassajara Road. Turn right and drive 1.3 miles to a signed Y-junction with Cachagua Road. Curve left and continue 5.1 miles to a cattle guard at the national forest boundary by barns and corrals on the right (west). Drive 0.2 miles further to the second gate opening on the left at the south end of Bruce Flat, a flat grassy meadow. Park in the pull-out on the left.

Hiking directions: Walk through the unsigned trailhead gate and cross the open meadow. Pass through a second trail gate and enter the forest. Descend the hillside, dropping 800 feet in the first 0.8 miles to an unsigned junction. The junction is near the transient stream in bucolic Anastasia Canyon. The Anastasia Trail continues left to Carmel Valley Road. Leave the Anastasia Trail and follow the shaded canyon floor to the right, parallel to the stream on the left. Pass moss covered tree trunks and rocks. Gradually ascend the hillside as the footpath becomes an old jeep road. Cross the creek at a horseshoe bend in the trail, and ascend the east slope of the canyon, weaving up to the ridge. Leave Anastasia Canyon and descend into Bear Trap Canyon. Curve sharply to the left, crossing a stream-fed draw.

Continue downhill to Cahoon Spring in a shady oak grove. The spring flows from a pipe near a clawfoot bathtub used as a horse trough. Climb a quarter mile up the canyon to The Bear Trap, an open ridge with panoramic views and an unsigned junction. The left fork leads to Carmel Valley Road, and the right fork leads to Tassajara Road. This is our turnaround spot. Return by retracing your steps.

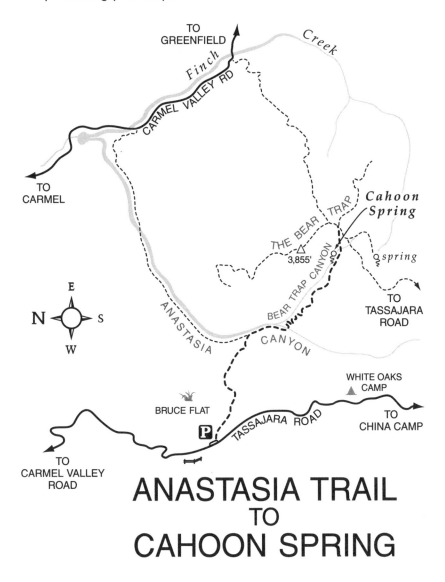

ANASTASIA TRAIL
TO
CAHOON SPRING

Hike 54
Pine Ridge Trail to Church Creek Divide

Hiking distance: 7.2 miles round trip
Hiking time: 3.5 hours
Elevation gain: 1,200 feet
Maps: U.S.G.S. Chews Ridge
      Ventana Wilderness Map

Summary of hike: Church Creek Divide sits in a shady tree grove of stately black and tanbark oaks, ponderosa pines and madrones. The divide, in a 1000-foot deep cleft below two ridges, is a major crossroad of several wilderness trails. This hike begins at the northeast end of the Pine Ridge Trail on a saddle above China Camp. The path weaves through the remote and rugged wilderness along high ridges with open grassy slopes. Panoramic views of the mountainous interior extend to Cone Peak, Junipero Serra Peak and down the Church Creek canyon.

Driving directions: From Highway 1 in Carmel, take Carmel Valley Road and drive 23 miles southeast (passing through Carmel Valley Village at 11.5 miles) to Tassajara Road. Turn right and drive 1.3 miles to a signed Y-junction with Cachagua Road. Curve left and continue 9.2 miles (crossing Chews Ridge) to the signed China Camp turnoff on the right. Continue 50 yards past the turnoff to the parking area on the left.

Hiking directions: Cross Tassajara Road to the posted Pine Ridge Trail. Climb the hillside above China Camp through native chaparral and brush. Burned oak and pine stumps remain from the 1977 Marble Cone Fire. After gaining 400 feet to a hilltop ridge, drop back down the hillside, losing the elevation gain on a long saddle in a stand of tanbark oaks. Cross a steep, sloping meadow just below the ridge and high above the Church Creek drainage. Traverse the hillside overlooking the sandstone formations in Church Creek Canyon to the left. Zigzag down the hillside to the canyon floor at Church Creek Divide. The divide sits in a pastoral forest by a posted 4-way junction. This is our turnaround spot.

To hike further, the Pine Ridge Trail continues straight ahead to Divide Camp at a half mile and eventually to Pfeiffer Big Sur State Park (Hike 36). To the right, the Carmel River Trail leads 2 miles to Pine Valley Camp, a flat grassy meadow lined with pines. The left fork follows Church Creek Canyon, passing the massive sandstone formations, to Wildcat Camp 5.7 miles ahead and Tassajara Road at 7 miles.

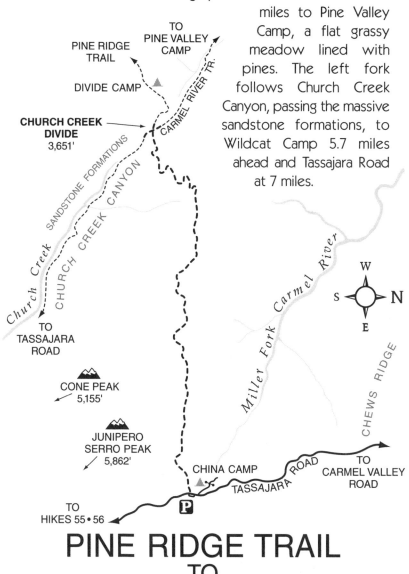

PINE RIDGE TRAIL
TO
CHURCH CREEK DIVIDE

Hike 55
Horse Pasture Trail
to Horse Pasture Camp

Hiking distance: 2.8 miles round trip
Hiking time: 1.5 hours
Elevation gain: 400 feet
Maps: U.S.G.S. Tassajara Hot Springs
　　　　　Ventana Wilderness Map

Summary of hike: Horse Pasture Trail is a lightly traveled trail off of Tassajara Road. The trail eventually leads to Willow Creek, linking Tassajara Road with Arroyo Seco. This hike leads to Horse Pasture Camp, a quiet, out-of-use campsite on the banks of seasonal Horse Pasture Creek. The camp sits on a beautiful creekside flat inside the Ventana Wilderness boundary.

Driving directions: From Highway 1 in Carmel, take Carmel Valley Road and drive 23 miles southeast (passing through Carmel Valley Village at 11.5 miles) to Tassajara Road. Turn right and drive 1.3 miles to a signed Y-junction with Cachagua Road. Curve left and continue 14.3 miles to the well-marked trailhead on the left (east) side. Park in the pullouts on either side of the road.

Hiking directions: Take the signed Horse Pasture Trail into the oak forest and head uphill. Traverse the hillside on a ledge above Tassajara Road. Curving away from the road, cross open grasslands on the narrow path. The gentle grade gains 400 feet in 0.6 miles, reaching a saddle at the wilderness boundary. Descend the east-facing slope under a canopy of oaks and toyon. Switchbacks lead down the hillside into the forested canyon and to seasonal Horse Pasture Creek. Cross the creek and walk downstream a short distance to the abandoned Horse Pasture Camp on a grassy flat. This is a good turnaround spot for a shorter 2.8-mile hike. To hike to Tassajara Creek or Willow Creek, continue with the following hike.

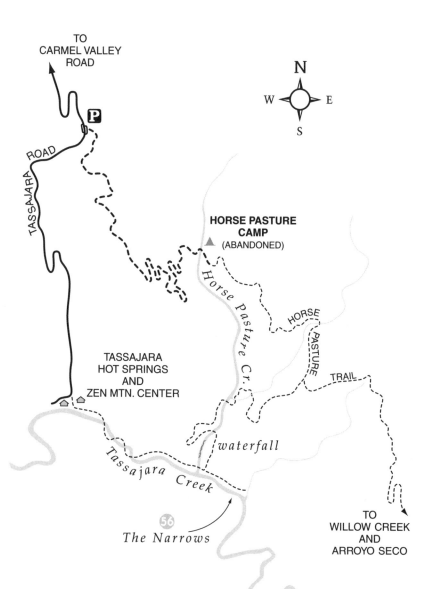

TO
CARMEL VALLEY
ROAD

P

TASSAJARA ROAD

N
W E
S

**HORSE PASTURE
CAMP**
(ABANDONED)

Horse Pasture Cr.

HORSE PASTURE TRAIL

TASSAJARA
HOT SPRINGS
AND
ZEN MTN. CENTER

waterfall

Tassajara Creek

56

The Narrows

TO
WILLOW CREEK
AND
ARROYO SECO

HORSE PASTURE TRAIL
TO CAMP

Hike 56
Horse Pasture Trail
to the Narrows at Tassajara Creek

Hiking distance: 7 miles round trip
Hiking time: 3.5 hours
Elevation gain: 1,200 feet
Maps: U.S.G.S. Tassajara Hot Springs
   Ventana Wilderness Map

Summary of hike: This hike leads to The Narrows on Tassajara Creek, a series of gorgeous pools and small waterfalls in a narrow canyon. This hike begins on the Horse Pasture Trail and descends down a side canyon, passing a waterfall in a rocky gorge. Upstream from The Narrows is Tassajara Hot Springs, located on the monastic Zen Mountain Center grounds.

Driving directions: Same as Hike 55.

Hiking directions: From the abandoned Horse Pasture Camp—where Hike 55 leaves off—follow the near-level path through grasslands with oak groves. Cross a shady stream-fed gully lined with ferns. Gradually ascend the hillside, curving right in the seasonal drainage at 2 miles. Continue 0.3 miles to a posted junction. The left fork continues on the Horse Pasture Trail to Willow Creek and Arroyo Seco. Take the right fork on the Tassajara Cut-Off Trail. Descend into the lush draw, winding into the small side canyon. Cross a rocky streambed at 2.8 miles, and parallel the stream. Recross the stream and follow the watercourse along its left bank. Cross Horse Pasture Creek, passing large boulders to an overlook in a rocky gorge at the brink of a waterfall. The narrow, rocky path steeply descends along the canyon wall to a posted T-junction at Tassajara Creek. The left fork follows the creek 100 yards downstream, passing a series of pools and small waterfalls called The Narrows. The right fork follows the creek upstream past more pools. After several creek crossings, the trail ends at the Tassajara Zen Mountain Center near the south end of Tassajara Road. After enjoying the

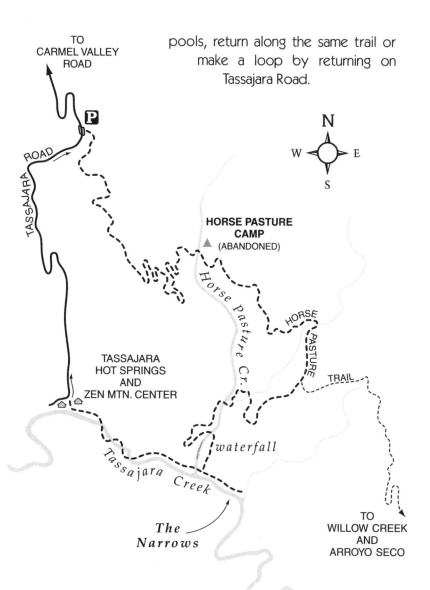

pools, return along the same trail or make a loop by returning on Tassajara Road.

TO
CARMEL VALLEY
ROAD

P

TASSAJARA ROAD

N
W · E
S

HORSE PASTURE CAMP (ABANDONED)

Horse Pasture Cr.

HORSE PASTURE

TRAIL

TASSAJARA
HOT SPRINGS
AND
ZEN MTN. CENTER

Tassajara Creek

waterfall

The Narrows

TO
WILLOW CREEK
AND
ARROYO SECO

HORSE PASTURE TRAIL
TO
THE NARROWS

Hike 57
Rocky Creek Trail to Rocky Creek Camp

Hiking distance: 4.8 miles round trip
Hiking time: 2.5 hours
Elevation gain: 600 feet
Maps: U.S.G.S. Junipero Serra Peak and Tassajara Hot Springs
Ventana Wilderness Map

Summary of hike: The Rocky Creek Trail begins in the Arroyo Seco Campground and follows the north canyon wall above the Arroyo Seco to Rocky Creek. The path winds up the narrow Rocky Creek drainage through scattered groves of oaks, buckeyes, madrones, maples, manzanitas and sycamores. After several creek crossings, the trail reaches Rocky Creek Camp, which sits on a 6-foot terrace above Rocky Creek and a tributary stream.

Driving directions: From Highway 1 in Carmel, take Carmel Valley Road and drive 40 miles southeast (passing through Carmel Valley Village at 11.5 miles) to Arroyo Seco Road. Turn right and drive 4.6 miles to the Arroyo Seco Campground entrance. The posted trailhead is on the right (north) side of the entrance kiosk. Drive 60 yards ahead, crossing the bridge over the Arroyo Seco, to the day use parking lot on the right. A parking fee is required.

To access the campground from Soledad/Highway 101, follow the driving directions to Hike 58.

Hiking directions: Walk back down the road, and cross the bridge over the Arroyo Seco. Bear left on the short, paved driveway by the campground entrance station. The posted footpath heads up the slope and curves west. Traverse the open hillside overlooking the multi-layered campground and the pools along the Arroyo Seco. At 1 mile, curve northwest into Rocky Creek Canyon. Follow the east wall of the side canyon past bedrock outcroppings, gradually descending to Rocky Creek. Cross Rocky Creek six times as the tree-shaded canyon narrows. After the sixth crossing, climb up the south-facing hillside, and descend to a grassy flat in an open oak grove. Wind through the flat to Rocky Creek just above its confluence with a tributary stream. Cross the creek and enter the posted Rocky Creek Camp, bordered by both streams. Return along the same trail.

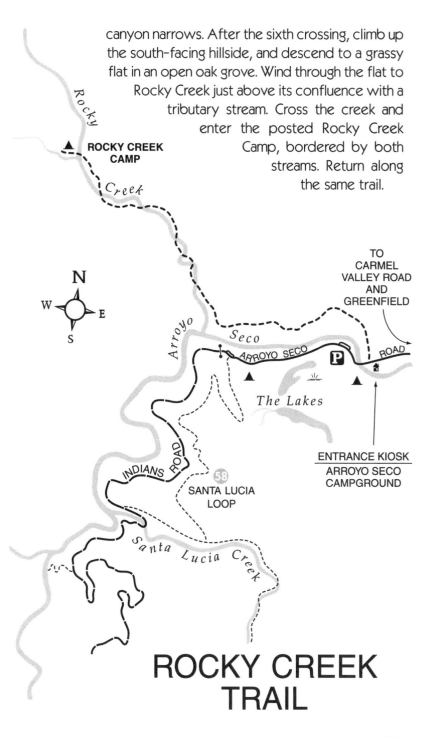

ROCKY CREEK TRAIL

Hike 58
Santa Lucia Loop

Hiking distance: 4.5 mile loop
Hiking time: 2.5 hours
Elevation gain: 300 feet
Maps: U.S.G.S. Junipero Serra Peak
Ventana Wilderness Map

Summary of hike: The Santa Lucia Loop traverses a steep mountain slope high above the scenic Arroyo Seco Gorge. The trail begins at the Arroyo Seco Campground and leads to the Santa Lucia Adobe, an adobe brick building with a cobblestone foundation built in 1908. The restored adobe, a ranger station until the late 1920s, resides on the banks of Santa Lucia Creek.

Driving directions: From Salinas, drive 27 miles south on Highway 101 to the Arroyo Seco Road exit in Soledad. Turn right and drive 20.8 miles (passing Carmel Valley Road at 16.2 miles) to the Arroyo Seco Campground entrance. Enter the campground and drive 0.7 miles to the posted Santa Lucia Trail on the left. Park in the day use lot on the right, across from the trail. A parking fee is required.

To access the campground from Carmel Valley Road and Carmel, follow the driving directions to Hike 57.

Hiking directions: Cross the campground road to the posted trail. Ascend the hillside above the upper campground through a forest of oak and buckeye. A short distance up the hill is a view of the north lake. Curve sharply right and climb to the ridge with a view of the southern lake. Curve left and follow the narrow cliffside path overlooking the magnificent Arroyo Seco Gorge and Indians Road, our return route. Traverse the steep slope, contouring along the level hillside path to a saddle by an old wire fence. Descend into an oak studded meadow to an old unpaved road above Santa Lucia Creek. Bear left on the road, and head 150 yards downhill to the Santa Lucia Adobe on the banks of the creek. The Santa Lucia Trail continues past the adobe and climbs to the head of the canyon. For this hike, return back up the road, passing the Santa Lucia Trail junction, to the Arroyo Seco/Indians Road. Bear right and follow the serpentine gorge for 2 miles on the narrow, unpaved road. Complete the loop at the parking area.

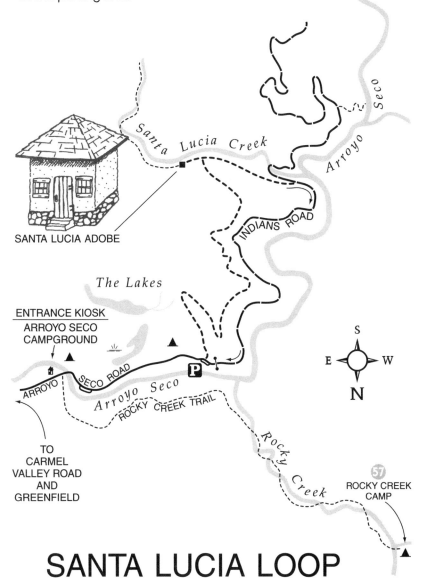

SANTA LUCIA ADOBE

The Lakes

ENTRANCE KIOSK
ARROYO SECO
CAMPGROUND

TO
CARMEL
VALLEY ROAD
AND
GREENFIELD

ROCKY CREEK
CAMP

SANTA LUCIA LOOP

Hike 59
Hare Creek Trail
Limekiln State Park

Hiking distance: 0.9 miles round trip
Hiking time: 30 minutes
Elevation gain: 150 feet
Maps: U.S.G.S. Lopez Point
       Limekiln State Park map

Summary of hike: Limekiln State Park is a magnificent 716-acre park and campground. Three year-round creeks flow through the park under the shade of towering coastal redwoods with a lush mix of sycamores, oaks and maples. Hare Creek is a tributary stream that feeds Limekiln Creek within the dense forest. The trail begins at the mouth of Limekiln Canyon. It then follows Hare Creek up the narrow canyon past clusters of redwoods, small waterfalls and continuous cascades. The trail once followed Hare Canyon up to Vicente Flat (Hikes 63 and 64). The trail now ends at the park boundary.

Driving directions: From the Big Sur Ranger Station, located 27 miles south of Carmel, drive 25.3 miles south on Highway 1 to the signed Limekiln State Park. Turn left (inland) to the entrance kiosk. Park 30 yards ahead in the day use parking area on the right. An entrance fee is required.
    From Highway 1 at Ragged Point, located 1.5 miles south of the Monterey County line, drive 22.2 miles north to the state park on the right.

Hiking directions: Walk up the campground road to the road's north end near the confluence of Limekiln Creek and Hare Creek. Cross the footbridge over Hare Creek in a dense redwood forest. At the posted trail fork, the left fork parallels Limekiln Creek to the waterfall and limekilns (Hikes 60 and 61). Take the right fork and head up the shady side canyon along the north bank of the creek. Follow the narrow, rock-walled canyon on a gentle uphill grade, passing continuous cascades and small waterfalls. The trail ends by a beautiful cascade and an 8-foot waterfall. Return along the same route.

Back at the trailhead, walk down the campground road. Cross the bridge over Limekiln Creek to the small crescent-shaped beach with offshore rocks. Limekiln Creek flows into the ocean, bisecting the sandy beach cove surrounded by steep rock walls.

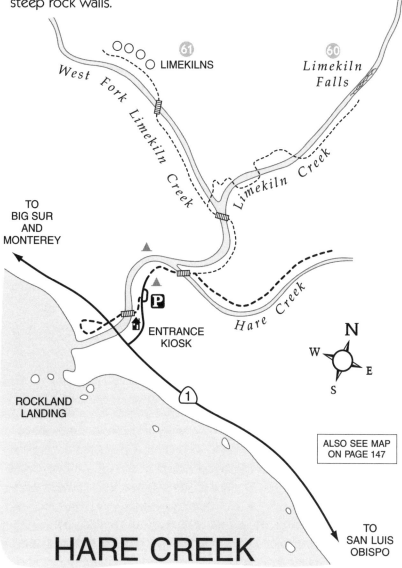

ALSO SEE MAP
ON PAGE 147

Hike 60
Waterfall Trail
Limekiln State Park

Hiking distance: 1.3 miles round trip
Hiking time: 30 minutes
Elevation gain: 200 feet
Maps: U.S.G.S. Lopez Point
Limekiln State Park map

Summary of hike: Limekiln Falls cascades 100 feet off a vertical limestone wall and fans out more than 25-feet wide. This trail meanders through a stunning redwood forest, following the cascading watercourse of Limekiln Creek to the base of the majestic cataract in a narrow box canyon.

Driving directions: From the Big Sur Ranger Station, located 27 miles south of Carmel, drive 25.3 miles south on Highway 1 to the signed Limekiln State Park. Turn left (inland) to the entrance kiosk. Park 30 yards ahead in the day use parking area on the right. An entrance fee is required.

From Highway 1 at Ragged Point, located 1.5 miles south of the Monterey County line, drive 22.2 miles north to the state park on the right.

Hiking directions: Walk up the campground road to the road's north end near the confluence of Limekiln Creek and Hare Creek. Cross the footbridge over Hare Creek in a dense redwood forest to a posted trail fork. The right fork parallels Hare Creek (Hike 59). Take the left fork, following the contours of Limekiln Creek through the shady redwood forest. Cross a second footbridge where Limekiln Creek and the West Fork flow together. Seventy yards past the bridge is a posted junction. The left fork continues to the limekilns along the West Fork (Hike 61). Take the right fork down log steps, and boulder hop across the West Fork. Head up the side canyon, and cross Limekiln Creek to its east bank. Pass a magnificent triple-trunk redwood tree, and head upstream past endless cascades, pools and small waterfalls. After crossing the creek two more times, the path reaches the end of the lush canyon at the base of the waterfall. Return along the same trail.

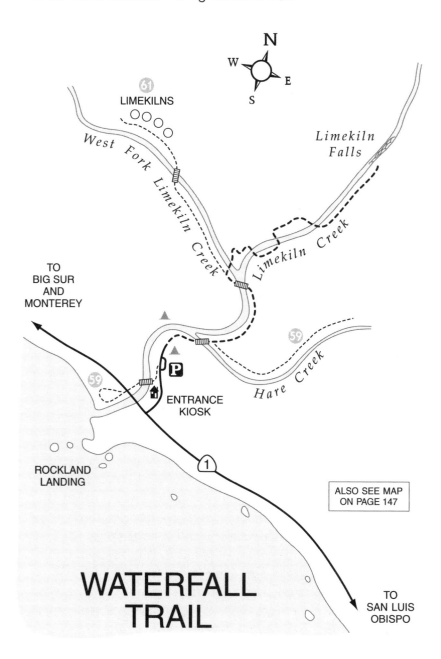

N
W · E
S

LIMEKILNS

West Fork Limekiln Creek

Limekiln Falls

Limekiln Creek

TO
BIG SUR
AND
MONTEREY

Hare Creek

P

ENTRANCE
KIOSK

ROCKLAND
LANDING

1

ALSO SEE MAP
ON PAGE 147

WATERFALL
TRAIL

TO
SAN LUIS
OBISPO

Hike 61
Redwood Trail to the Limekilns
Limekiln State Park

Hiking distance: 1 mile round trip
Hiking time: 30 minutes
Elevation gain: 200 feet
Maps: U.S.G.S. Lopez Point
Limekiln State Park map

Summary of hike: The Limekiln Trail leads to four massive stone and steel kilns used to purify quarried limestone into powdered lime in the 1880s. The lime was used as an ingredient in cement. The Limekiln Trail follows the old wagon route used to haul barrels of lime slacked from the furnaces. The hike follows Limekiln Creek and the West Fork up the canyon through redwoods, sycamores, oaks and maples to the giant limekilns.

Driving directions: From the Big Sur Ranger Station, located 27 miles south of Carmel, drive 25.3 miles south on Highway 1 to the signed Limekiln State Park. Turn left (inland) to the entrance kiosk. Park 30 yards ahead in the day use parking area on the right. An entrance fee is required.

From Highway 1 at Ragged Point, located 1.5 miles south of the Monterey County line, drive 22.2 miles north to the state park on the right.

Hiking directions: Walk up the campground road to the road's north end near the confluence of Limekiln Creek and Hare Creek. Cross the footbridge over Hare Creek in the dense redwood forest to a posted trail fork. The right fork parallels Hare Creek (Hike 59). Take the left fork, following the contours of Limekiln Creek through the shady redwood forest. Cross a second footbridge where Limekiln Creek and the West Fork flow together. Follow the west bank of the West Fork, passing the Waterfall Trail on the right (Hike 60). Continue to a third bridge by cascades and a small waterfall. Head gradually uphill along the east side of the creek, skirting past a large rock outcropping. Thirty yards beyond the rock are the four enormous metal cylinders on the right. On the left are waterfalls and pools. Return by retracing your steps.

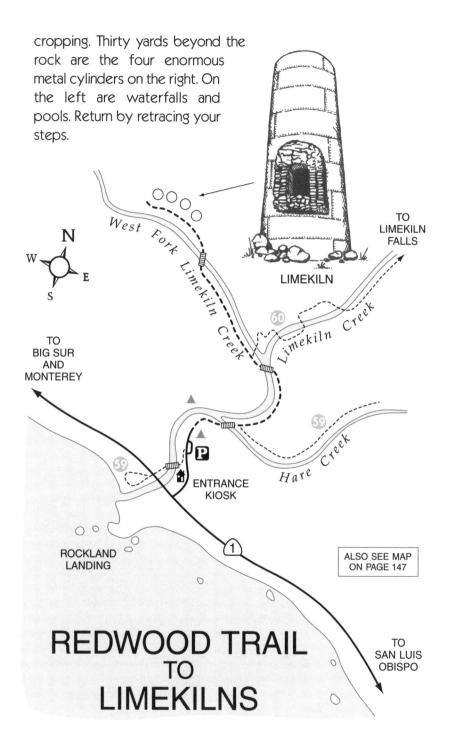

LIMEKILN

TO LIMEKILN FALLS

TO BIG SUR AND MONTEREY

West Fork Limekiln Creek

Limekiln Creek

Hare Creek

60

59

59

ENTRANCE KIOSK

ROCKLAND LANDING

1

ALSO SEE MAP ON PAGE 147

TO SAN LUIS OBISPO

REDWOOD TRAIL
TO
LIMEKILNS

Hike 62
Kirk Creek Beach

Hiking distance: 0.5 miles round trip
Hiking time: 30 minutes
Elevation gain: 150 feet
Maps: U.S.G.S. Cape San Martin
　　　Los Padres National Forest Northern Section Trail Map

Summary of hike: Kirk Creek Campground sits on the bluffs overlooking the ocean with magnificent views north to Lopez Point. The trail to the beach crosses the grassy marine terrace to dramatic eroded cliffs and rock formations. The path descends the cliffs to a small sandy beach cove with scattered boulders.

Driving directions: From the Big Sur Ranger Station, located 27 miles south of Carmel, drive 27.2 miles south on Highway 1 to the Kirk Creek Campground on the right (ocean) side. Park in the campground day use lot (entrance fee required) or in the pullouts along the highway (free).
　　From Highway 1 at Ragged Point, 1.5 miles south of the Monterey County line, drive 20.4 miles north to Kirk Creek Campground on the left. The campground is 4.4 miles north of the Pacific Valley Ranger Station.

Hiking directions: Follow the campground road to the north end of the camp. The signed trail is by campsite 23. Follow the signed grassy path past the picnic area and through the grove of eucalyptus trees on the bluffs. Descend along the edge of the cliffs. Switchbacks lead down to the small, sandy beach cove. The last 50 feet are a scramble due to erosion. After exploring the cove, return on the same path.

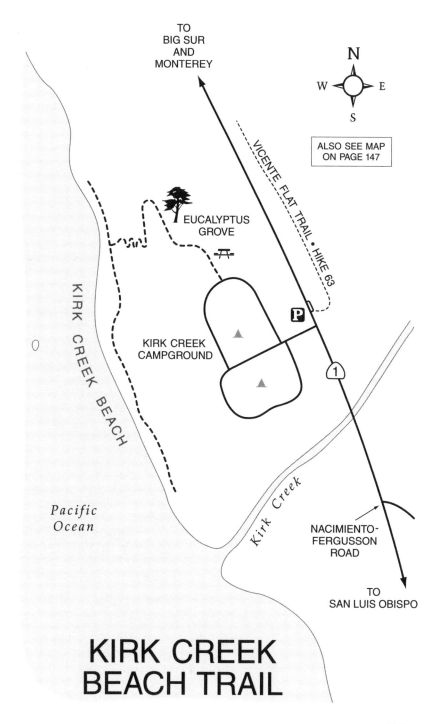

TO
BIG SUR
AND
MONTEREY

N
W — E
S

ALSO SEE MAP
ON PAGE 147

VICENTE FLAT TRAIL • HIKE 63

EUCALYPTUS
GROVE

P

KIRK CREEK
CAMPGROUND

KIRK CREEK BEACH

1

Kirk Creek

Pacific
Ocean

NACIMIENTO-
FERGUSSON
ROAD

TO
SAN LUIS OBISPO

KIRK CREEK
BEACH TRAIL

Hike 63
Vicente Flat Trail
from Kirk Creek Campground

Hiking distance: 10.6 miles round trip

**map
next page**

Hiking time: 6 hours
Elevation gain: 1,700 feet
Maps: U.S.G.S. Cape San Martin and Cone Peak
      Ventana Wilderness Map

Summary of hike: Vicente Flat is a large, beautiful camp on the banks of Hare Creek. The camp sits in a grove of majestic redwoods and a sunny meadow the size of a football field. The Vicente Flat Trail (also called Kirk Creek Trail) is one of the most scenic and diverse hikes in the Ventana Wilderness. The trail begins at the coast and crosses scrub covered coastal slopes above Pacific Valley, with sweeping ocean views. The trail leads to Hare Canyon, where the path follows the south wall of the canyon into wood-shaded ravines and meadowlands. The trail reaches Hare Creek under a canopy of towering redwoods. This hike can be combined with Hike 64 for a 7.4-mile, one-way downhill shuttle hike (starting from Cone Peak Road).

Driving directions: From the Big Sur Ranger Station, located 27 miles south of Carmel, drive 27.2 miles south on Highway 1 to the Kirk Creek Campground on the right. The posted trail is on the left, directly across from the campground. Park in a pull-out alongside the highway.

From Highway 1 at Ragged Point, 1.5 miles south of the Monterey County line, drive 20.4 miles north to the Kirk Creek Campground and trailhead.

Hiking directions: Climb the exposed, brush covered coastal slope toward the saddle, while the magnificent coastal views from above Pacific Valley improve with every step. Just before reaching the saddle, bear left and cross the sloping grassland to the posted wilderness boundary. Cross a gully below the sheer rock cliffs, and curve west to the west tip of the ridge, with sweeping panoramas from north to south. Climb the ridge and curve north. Traverse the upper mountain slope, wending in and out of mature redwood and bay groves. Contour around three more sizeable gullies to the south wall of Hare Canyon at 3 miles. The views extend up Limekiln Canyon and Hare Canyon to Cone Peak. Curve east and follow the level path through redwood groves along the south wall of Hare Canyon. Continue to Espinosa Camp on a little shoulder to the left. The camp is 20 yards off the trail on a flat, grassy ridge with an ocean view. A quarter mile after the camp, cross a redwood-lined stream. Continue through the forest on a moderate grade for 2 miles, then begin a steady descent to Hare Creek on the canyon floor. Cross the creek to a posted junction with the Stone Ridge Trail on the left. Bear to the right and enter Vicente Flat. Campsites line the creek among the towering redwoods. Return along the same trail.

Vicente Flat is also the destination for Hike 64. For a one-way shuttle hike, begin the hike from Cone Peak Road—Hike 64—and continue 7.4 miles down to the Kirk Creek Campground.

Hike 64
Vicente Flat Trail from Cone Peak Road

Hiking distance: 4.5 miles round trip
Hiking time: 3 hours
Elevation gain: 1,600 feet
Maps: U.S.G.S. Cone Peak
       Ventana Wilderness Map

map
next page

Summary of hike: Vicente Flat is a spacious camp with a large open meadow along the banks of Hare Creek. Campsites line the serene, streamside glade under a canopy of majestic redwoods. The well-graded Vicente Flat Trail descends from its upper east end at Cone Peak Road. The path drops into wooded Hare Canyon, with exceptional views to the sea down the 3,000-foot deep canyon. The downhill path parallels Hare Creek beneath the shade of massive redwoods. This trail may be combined with Hike 63 for a 7.4-mile, one-way down-hill shuttle hike.

Driving directions: From the Big Sur Ranger Station, located 27 miles south of Carmel, drive 27.4 miles south to Nacimiento-Fergusson Road. The road is 0.2 miles south of Kirk Creek Campground. Turn inland and wind up the paved mountain road 7.1 miles to the South Coast Ridge Road on the right. Turn left on the narrow, unpaved Central Coast Ridge Road (also known as Cone Peak Road), and drive 3.7 miles to the posted trail on the left. Park in the pullout on the left, just past the trailhead. Cone Peak Road is impassable in wet weather.

From Highway 1 at Ragged Point, 1.5 miles south of the Monterey County line, drive 20.2 miles north to Nacimiento-Fergusson Road, located 4.2 miles north of the Pacific Valley Ranger Station.

Hiking directions: Walk up the hill and curve around to the south side of the knoll. Descend from the head of Hare Canyon. At a quarter mile, the path steeply zigzags down the south wall of the canyon and temporarily levels out on a small grassy ridge. Curve to the right and continue down switchbacks to Hare Creek in the shaded redwood grove. Follow the creek downstream through lush riparian vegetation, climbing over and stooping under a few fallen redwoods while crossing Hare Creek five times. The fifth crossing is at the upper reaches of Vicente Flat, with campsites on each side of the creek. Stroll through the dense grove of redwoods along the west side of the creek to the heart of Vicente Flat by a grassy meadow. A lower path borders the creek to several campsites. Just beyond the meadow is a posted junction, our turnaround spot. The Vicente Flat Trail bears to the left and descends 5 miles to Highway 1 at Kirk Creek Campground. The Stone Ridge Trail, straight ahead on the right fork, leads to Goat Camp and the Gamboa Trail.

To hike the 7.4-mile shuttle hike, continue on the Vicente Flat Trail down to the Kirk Creek Campground—Hike 63.

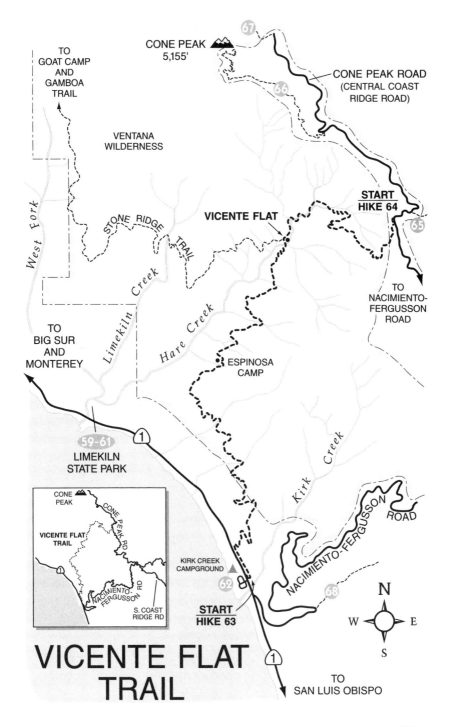

TO
GOAT CAMP
AND
GAMBOA
TRAIL

CONE PEAK
5,155'

67

CONE PEAK ROAD
(CENTRAL COAST
RIDGE ROAD)

66

VENTANA
WILDERNESS

STONE RIDGE TRAIL

West Fork

Limekiln Creek

VICENTE FLAT

START
HIKE 64

65

TO
NACIMIENTO-
FERGUSSON
ROAD

Hare Creek

ESPINOSA
CAMP

TO
BIG SUR
AND
MONTEREY

59-61

1

LIMEKILN
STATE PARK

Kirk Creek

NACIMIENTO-FERGUSSON ROAD

CONE
PEAK

VICENTE FLAT
TRAIL

CONE PEAK RD

NACIMIENTO-
FERGUSSON RD

S. COAST
RIDGE RD

KIRK CREEK
CAMPGROUND

62

START
HIKE 63

68

N
W   E
S

VICENTE FLAT
TRAIL

1

TO
SAN LUIS OBISPO

Hike 65
San Antonio Trail to Fresno Camp

Hiking distance: 3 miles round trip
Hiking time: 2 hours
Elevation gain: 1,000 feet
Maps: U.S.G.S. Cone Peak
       Ventana Wilderness Map

Summary of hike: Fresno Camp is a large, picturesque camp on the floor of the San Antonio River canyon. The lush camp stretches along the San Antonio River in a wide meadow under a broad mix of trees. The trail, which receives minimal use, begins on the dry, brush covered hillside and descends through groves of oak and bay trees to the verdant, stream-fed camp.

Driving directions: Parking is not available at the San Antonio Trailhead. Park in the Vicente Flat Trailhead parking pullout, following the directions for Hike 64.

Hiking directions: Walk up the road 0.15 miles to the brown trail sign on the right. Take the footpath along the north canyon wall, entering the Ventana Wilderness. The narrow path skirts through the brush, reaching a saddle at a quarter mile. Descend from the saddle along the south wall of the San Antonio River drainage under the shadow of Cone Peak, entering groves of oaks, bays and young madrone trees. Follow a gentle downhill grade along the contours of the hillside with sweeping mountain views to the north and west. Three short switchbacks drop down to the San Antonio River and Fresno Camp in a large grassy flat at 1.5 miles. The large terraced campsite stretches along the river on the canyon floor under sycamores, ponderosa pine, oaks and maples. The upper camp sits under the shade of maple trees. This is our turnaround spot.

To hike further, the trail crosses the river at the lower end of the camp and continues to San Antonio Camp, 2 miles ahead. However, the trail becomes hard to follow with fallen trees and heavy brush.

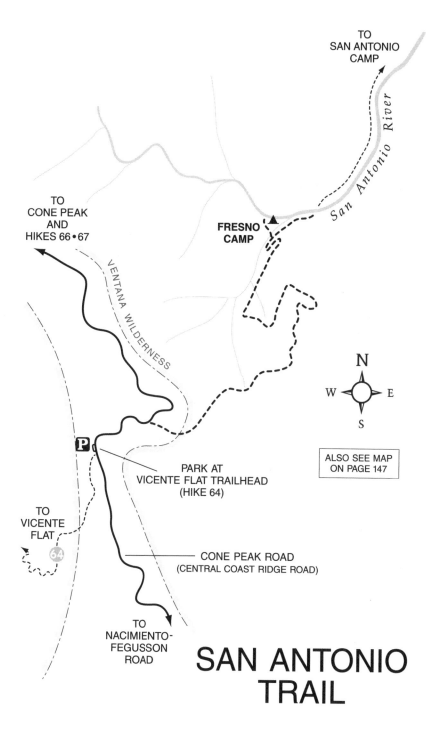

TO
SAN ANTONIO
CAMP

San Antonio River

TO
CONE PEAK
AND
HIKES 66 • 67

FRESNO
CAMP

VENTANA WILDERNESS

N
W E
S

ALSO SEE MAP
ON PAGE 147

P

PARK AT
VICENTE FLAT TRAILHEAD
(HIKE 64)

TO
VICENTE
FLAT

64

CONE PEAK ROAD
(CENTRAL COAST RIDGE ROAD)

TO
NACIMIENTO-
FEGUSSON
ROAD

SAN ANTONIO
TRAIL

Hike 66
Cone Peak Trail

Hiking distance: 4.6 miles round trip
Hiking time: 2.5 hours
Elevation gain: 1,400 feet
Maps: U.S.G.S. Cone Peak
        Ventana Wilderness Map

Summary of hike: Cone Peak rises nearly a mile high from the ocean in just over 3 miles. From the summit are spectacular 360-degree views of the deep blue ocean and the surrounding peaks and valleys of the Santa Lucia Range. This hike follows the moderate southern slope to the fire lookout atop the peak. The lookout is only occupied during the fire season.

Driving directions: From the Big Sur Ranger Station, located 27 miles south of Carmel, drive 27.4 miles south to Nacimiento-Fergusson Road. The road is 0.2 miles south of Kirk Creek Campground. Turn inland and wind up the paved mountain road 7.1 miles to the South Coast Ridge Road on the right. Turn left on the narrow, unpaved Central Coast Ridge Road (also known as Cone Peak Road), and drive 5.3 miles to the posted trail on the left. Park in the pullout on the left, just past the trailhead. Cone Peak Road is impassable in wet weather.

From Highway 1 at Ragged Point, 1.5 miles south of the Monterey County line, drive 20.2 miles north to Nacimiento-Fergusson Road, located 4.2 miles north of the Pacific Valley Ranger Station.

Hiking directions: Walk past the trailhead sign and ascend the hill. Three switchbacks lead a quarter mile to a spectacular view of the ocean, mountains and the lookout tower atop Cone Peak. Head north up the ridge through tall brush. Cross a saddle high above Hare Canyon and just below the ridge of Cone Peak. Traverse the mountain slope on the long, ascending grade dotted with Coulter pines, sugar pines and bays. A series of short, steep switchbacks climbs the mountain and crosses a ridge to a posted junction at 1.8 miles, just below the Cone Peak summit. The left fork drops steeply down the mountain to Trail Spring Camp. Stay to the right (east) and climb a quarter mile on steep switchbacks, passing rare Santa Lucia fir, to the lookout tower. After savoring the views, return along the same route.

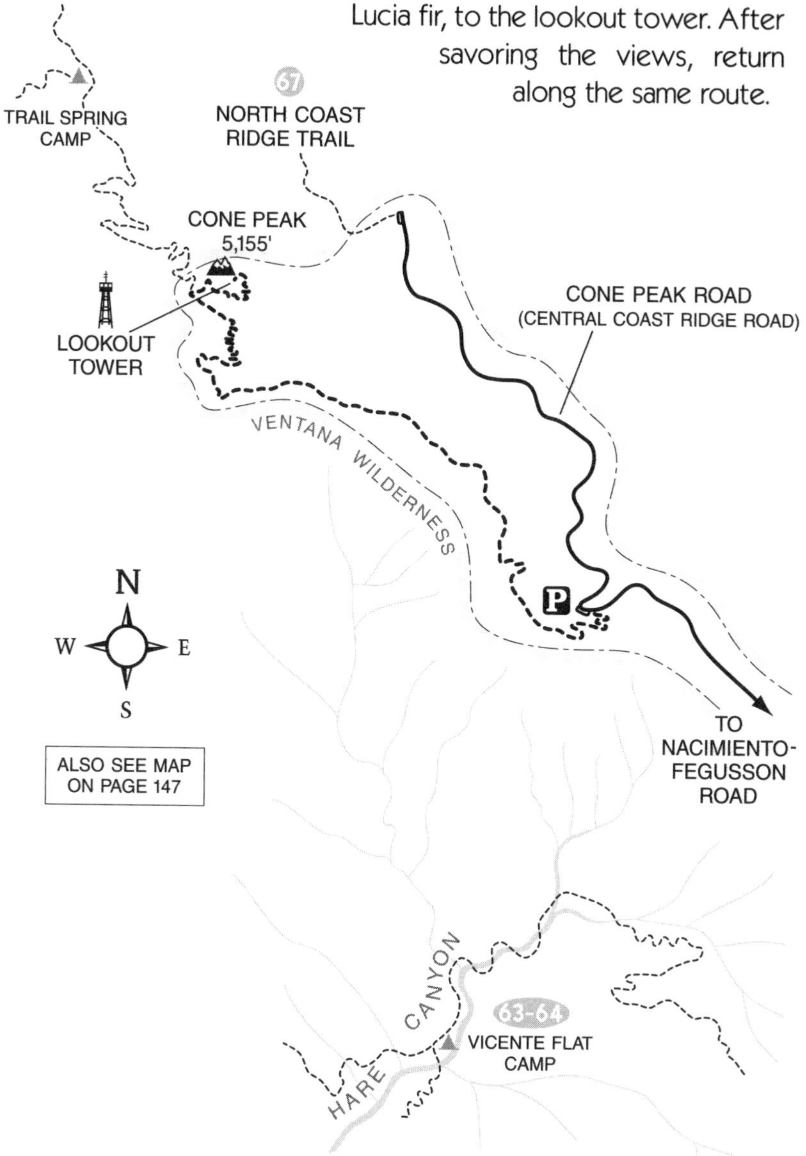

TRAIL SPRING
CAMP

NORTH COAST
RIDGE TRAIL

67

CONE PEAK
5,155'

CONE PEAK ROAD
(CENTRAL COAST RIDGE ROAD)

LOOKOUT
TOWER

VENTANA WILDERNESS

P

N

W · E

S

ALSO SEE MAP
ON PAGE 147

TO
NACIMIENTO-
FEGUSSON
ROAD

HARE CANYON

63-64

VICENTE FLAT
CAMP

CONE PEAK TRAIL

Hike 67
North Coast Ridge Trail to Cook Spring Camp

Hiking distance: 5 miles round trip
Hiking time: 3 hours
Elevation gain: 800 feet
Maps: U.S.G.S. Cone Peak and Lopez Point
      Ventana Wilderness Map

Summary of hike: The North Coast Ridge Trail begins along the north flank of Cone Peak and follows a craggy ridge with sweeping coastal and mountain views. This hike leads to Cook Spring Camp, a lightly used, multi-level camp with a small spring under a stand of old sugar pines.

Driving directions: Follow the driving directions for Hike 66. From the Cone Peak Trailhead, continue 1.3 miles on Cone Peak Road to the parking area at the end of the road.

Hiking directions: Take the old road along the north side of Cone Peak, and wind through craggy metamorphic rock in an open forest of towering pines. Cross a talus slope of fractured rock while overlooking the rugged canyon lands and layered ridges of the Santa Lucia Mountains. At a half mile the road narrows to a footpath and descends on two short switchbacks. Traverse the steep mountainside through a live oak forest, crossing several more talus slopes. Zigzag up six switchbacks to the head of the canyon, reaching the ridge where the lookout tower atop Cone Peak is in view. Pass a junction with the Gamboa Trail, and continue north along the coastal ridge, passing jagged rock formations to the saddle. Cross the crest to the east-facing slope in an old fire burned area, where the trail widens. Descend gradually to an unmarked, abandoned road on the right at 2 miles. Take the road and snake steeply downhill to the right, reaching Cook Spring Camp in a grove of huge sugar pines. The spring is to the west of the upper camp. Return to the North Coast Ridge Trail. Continue north less than a half mile to a garden of rounded sandstone boulders and an overlook at a hairpin left bend. Panoramic 360-degree views extend from the ocean to the Salinas Valley. Numerous side paths descend to the boulders. This is our turnaround spot.

To extend the hike, the trail continues to a junction with the Arroyo Seco Trail in just over a half mile.

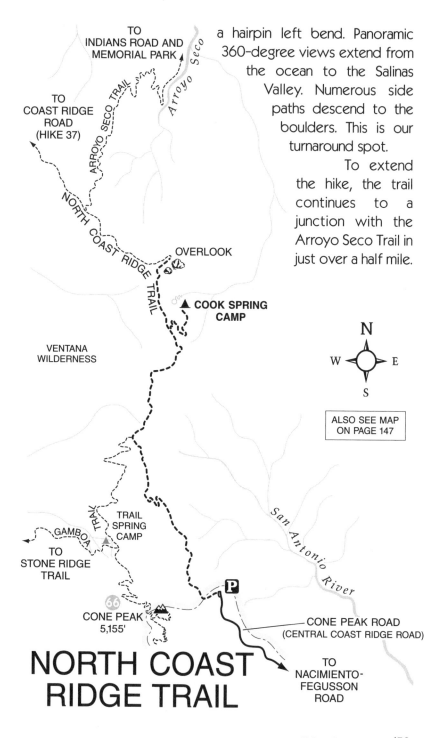

TO INDIANS ROAD AND MEMORIAL PARK

Arroyo Seco

ARROYO SECO TRAIL

TO COAST RIDGE ROAD (HIKE 37)

NORTH COAST RIDGE TRAIL

OVERLOOK

▲ COOK SPRING CAMP

VENTANA WILDERNESS

N
W — E
S

ALSO SEE MAP ON PAGE 147

GAMBOA TRAIL

TRAIL SPRING CAMP

TO STONE RIDGE TRAIL

San Antonio River

66

CONE PEAK 5,155'

P

CONE PEAK ROAD (CENTRAL COAST RIDGE ROAD)

TO NACIMIENTO-FERGUSSON ROAD

NORTH COAST RIDGE TRAIL

Hike 68
Mill Creek Trail

Hiking distance: 3 miles round trip
Hiking time: 2 hours
Elevation gain: 600 feet
Maps: U.S.G.S. Cape San Martin
        Ventana Wilderness Map

Summary of hike: The Mill Creek Trail follows the bucolic watershed up beautiful Mill Creek Canyon. The trail meanders alongside Mill Creek through riparian vegetation under the dark shade of giant redwoods, maples and sycamores. The hike ends at a campsite perched above the creek amidst a cluster of redwoods.

Driving directions: From the Big Sur Ranger Station, located 27 miles south of Carmel, drive 27.4 miles south on Highway 1 to Nacimiento-Fergusson Road. The road is 0.2 miles south of Kirk Creek Campground. Turn inland and wind up the paved mountain road 0.8 miles to the posted trail on the right, at a distinct left horseshoe bend. Park in the pullout on the right by the trailhead.
    From Highway 1 at Ragged Point, 1.5 miles south of the Monterey County line, drive 20.2 miles north to Nacimiento-Fergusson Road, located 4.2 miles north of the Pacific Valley Ranger Station.

Hiking directions: Climb 100 yards up the steep slope to a small saddle. Descend under a canopy of California bay laurel. The undulating path follows the north canyon wall high above Mill Creek. The creek can be heard but not yet seen, as towering redwoods carpet the canyon floor. Gradually drop down the hillside into a wet, lush forest of redwoods, maples, sycamores, bracken ferns and moss covered rocks at a half mile. Wind through the canyon, following the creek upstream. Rock hop over Lion Creek to a distinct but unmarked trail fork. Take the left fork and climb up a 15-foot slope. (The right fork ends 30 yards ahead.) Curve right, soon reaching a creek crossing. Rock hop over Mill Creek two consecutive times while passing waterfalls and pools. Scramble over a jumble of boulders at an old landslide, then follow a narrow ledge on the edge of the creek. The main trail curves to a plateau above the creek with a gorgeous campsite surrounded by a cluster of redwoods. This is our turn-around spot and a great place to explore the immediate surroundings. The trail continues up to the South Coast Ridge Road, but becomes indistinct just beyond camp.

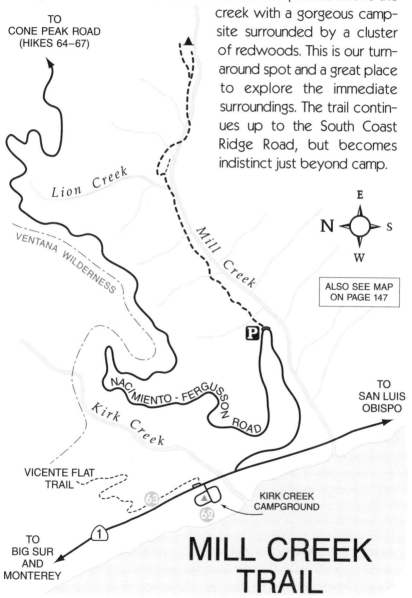

TO
CONE PEAK ROAD
(HIKES 64–67)

Lion Creek

VENTANA WILDERNESS

Mill Creek

E
N W S

ALSO SEE MAP
ON PAGE 147

P

NACIMIENTO-FERGUSSON ROAD

Kirk Creek

TO
SAN LUIS
OBISPO

VICENTE FLAT
TRAIL

63

KIRK CREEK
CAMPGROUND

62

1

TO
BIG SUR
AND
MONTEREY

MILL CREEK
TRAIL

Hike 69
Pacific Valley Flats

Hiking distance: 2 miles round trip
Hiking time: 1 hour
Elevation gain: 50 feet
Maps: U.S.G.S. Cape San Martin
          Los Padres National Forest Northern Section Trail Map

Summary of hike: Pacific Valley is a four-mile long, flat marine terrace. The wide expanse extends west from the steep slopes of the Santa Lucia Mountains to the serrated bluffs above the Pacific Ocean. This hike crosses the grassy coastal terrace to the eroded coastline a hundred feet above the ocean. There are dramatic views of Plaskett Rock, offshore rock formations with natural arches and the scalloped coastal cliffs. Numerous access points lead to the grassland terrace.

Driving directions: From the Big Sur Ranger Station, located 27 miles south of Carmel, drive 31.5 miles south on Highway 1 to the Pacific Valley Ranger Station on the left. The trailhead is across the highway from the ranger station. Park in the pullouts on either side of the road or in the parking lot at the station.

From Highway 1 at Ragged Point, 1.5 miles south of the Monterey County line, drive 16 miles north to the Pacific Valley Ranger Station.

Hiking directions: The hike begins directly across the road from the ranger station. Step up and over the trail access ladder. Head west across the grassy expanse and past rock outcroppings on the left. Near the point is a rolling sand dune on the right with numerous trails and great overlooks. The main trail stays to the north of the dune, leading to the edge of the cliffs along the jagged coastline high above the pounding surf. At one mile, the trail ends at a fenceline above Prewitt Creek. The trails around the dunes connect with the bluff trail south to Sand Dollar Beach (Hike 70), then circle back to the first junction at the cliff's edge. Return along the same trail.

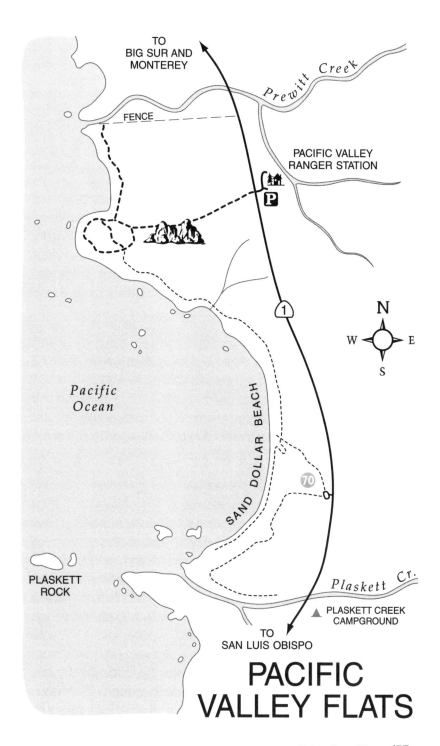

TO
BIG SUR AND
MONTEREY

Prewitt Creek

FENCE

PACIFIC VALLEY
RANGER STATION

P

1

N
W E
S

Pacific
Ocean

SAND DOLLAR BEACH

70

PLASKETT
ROCK

Plaskett Cr.

PLASKETT CREEK
CAMPGROUND

TO
SAN LUIS OBISPO

PACIFIC
VALLEY FLATS

Hike 70
Sand Dollar Beach

Hiking distance: 1.5 miles round trip
Hiking time: 1 hour
Elevation gain: 150 feet
Maps: U.S.G.S. Cape San Martin
          Los Padres National Forest Northern Section Trail Map

Summary of hike: Sand Dollar Beach is a protected horseshoe-shaped sand and rock beach between two rocky headlands. The trail passes a picnic area lined with cypress trees to the steep eroded cliffs and a cliffside overlook with interpretive signs. Plaskett Rock sits off the southern point. There are great coastal views of large offshore rock outcroppings. Cone Peak can be seen inland along the Santa Lucia Range.

Driving directions: From the Big Sur Ranger Station, located 27 miles south of Carmel, drive 32.4 miles south on Highway 1 to the parking lot on the right (ocean) side. Park in the lot (entrance fee) or park in the pullouts along the highway (free).

From Highway 1 at Ragged Point, 1.5 miles south of the Monterey County line, drive 15.1 miles north to the parking lot on the left, just north of Plaskett Creek Campground.

Hiking directions: The signed trailhead is at the north end of the parking lot. Walk up and over the stepladder, then descend through a shady picnic area. Cross the grasslands to a junction by a wooden fence. The right fork leads 30 yards to an overlook with an interpretive wildlife sign. Return to the junction and take the left fork down the switchbacks and a staircase to the shoreline. After exploring the crescent-shaped cove, return to the bluffs. An optional cliffside path heads one mile north to Pacific Valley (Hike 69).

From the Sand Dollar parking lot, a second trail leaves from the center of the lot. Climb up and over the ladder, and cross the grassy coastal terrace to a cliffside overlook. The meandering path follows the grassy bluffs less than a half mile south

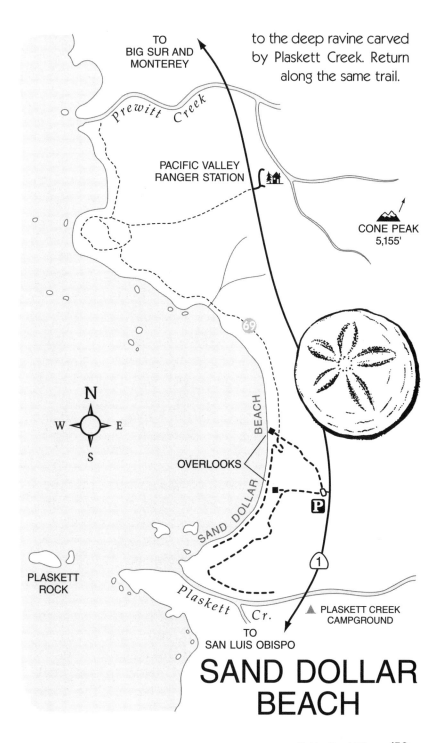

TO
BIG SUR AND
MONTEREY

to the deep ravine carved
by Plaskett Creek. Return
along the same trail.

Prewitt Creek

PACIFIC VALLEY
RANGER STATION

CONE PEAK
5,155'

N
W · E
S

BEACH

OVERLOOKS

SAND DOLLAR

P

PLASKETT
ROCK

Plaskett Cr.

1

PLASKETT CREEK
CAMPGROUND

TO
SAN LUIS OBISPO

SAND DOLLAR
BEACH

Hike 71
Jade Cove and Plaskett Rock

Hiking distance: 0.4 miles to 1.5 miles round trip
Hiking time: 30 to 60 minutes
Elevation gain: 150 feet
Maps: U.S.G.S. Cape San Martin

Summary of hike: Jade Cove is a small rocky cove with smooth ocean-tumbled stones and nephrite jade. The isolated cove sits at the base of steep 100-foot serpentine cliffs eroded by the rough surf. The trail crosses the grassy marine terrace to the edge of the cliffs, where the coastal views are spectacular. Cape San Martin extends out to sea to the south. Plaskett Rock, a dramatic outcropping, sits offshore to the north.

Driving directions: From the Big Sur Ranger Station, located 27 miles south of Carmel, drive 32.9 miles south on Highway 1 (0.4 miles south of Plaskett Creek Campground) to the Jade Cove Beach trailhead sign. There are pullouts on both sides of the highway.

From Highway 1 at Ragged Point, 1.5 miles south of the Monterey County line, drive 14.6 miles north (3 miles north of Gorda) to the signed trailhead.

Hiking directions: From the west (ocean) side of the highway, head over the access ladder. Continue down the steps, heading west across the wide, grassy terrace to the edge of the bluffs and a junction. To reach Jade Cove, zigzag down the steep, eroded cliffs. The descent is made easier with the help of switchbacks. Near the bottom, some boulder hopping is required to reach the shoreline. The path ends in Jade Cove amid the rounded stones. Return to the junction atop the bluffs.

To extend the hike, take the blufftop path to the north, skirting the edge of the cliffs a half mile to Plaskett Creek. A narrow path drops down the water-carved ravine to the creek. Another path follows the bluffs out on the headland that points toward Plaskett Rock. Return by retracing your path.

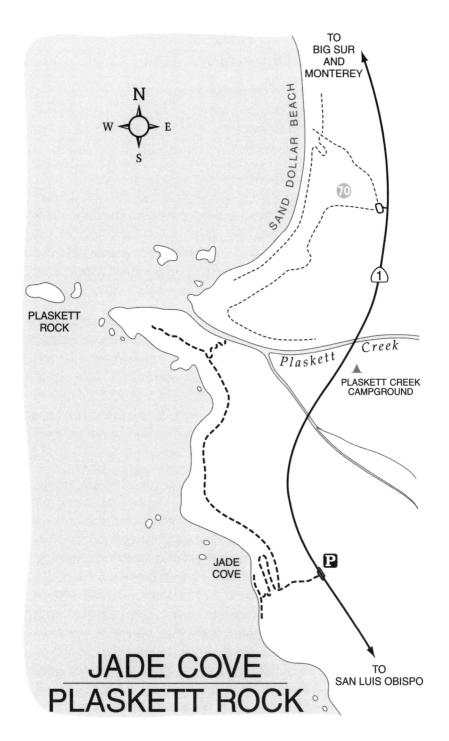

TO
BIG SUR
AND
MONTEREY

SAND DOLLAR BEACH

70

1

Plaskett Creek

PLASKETT CREEK
CAMPGROUND

PLASKETT
ROCK

JADE
COVE

P

JADE COVE
PLASKETT ROCK

TO
SAN LUIS OBISPO

Hike 72
Willow Creek Trail

Hiking distance: 3.4 miles round trip
Hiking time: 2 hours
Elevation gain: 500 feet
Maps: U.S.G.S. Cape San Martin
Los Padres National Forest Northern Section Trail Map

Summary of hike: The Willow Creek Trail is a little gem tucked between the Ventana Wilderness and the Silver Peak Wilderness. The unmarked and seldom hiked trail drops into an isolated stream-fed canyon under shady redwoods, oaks and maples. At Willow Creek is an old, rickety "Indiana Jones" style suspension bridge that spans 80 yards across the gorge.

Driving directions: From the Big Sur Ranger Station, 27 miles south of Carmel, drive 35 miles south to Willow Creek Road. It is located 2.5 miles south of Plaskett Creek Campground and just south of the Willow Creek bridge. Turn inland and wind up the narrow, unpaved mountain road 2.4 miles to an unsigned road junction on the left. This road—the Willow Creek Trail—no longer accommodates vehicles. Park in the pullout on the right, 40 yards before the junction.

From Highway 1 at Ragged Point, 1.5 miles south of the Monterey County line, drive 12.5 miles north to Willow Creek Road, 1 mile north of Gorda.

Hiking directions: Walk 60 yards up Willow Creek Road to the narrow, rutted road. Bear left and descend through the shade of pine and bay trees to an oak grove on a circular flat. Drop deeper into Willow Creek Canyon along the south canyon wall, passing a road on the left at 0.6 miles. The main road ends at 1 mile in a redwood grove, then continues as a footpath. Descend under the deep shade of the towering redwoods on the fern-lined path. Contour around a rocky, stream-fed gully, and traverse the lush hillside to an unmarked trail split. The left (lower) fork drops down to the creek at the dilapidated and unsafe suspension bridge spanning the gorge. To the left is a series of pools among a jumble of rocks. Back on the main trail, continue 0.15 miles to another unsigned trail fork. The left fork zigzags a short distance down to a campsite on a grassy flat perched 20 feet above Willow Creek. Back on the main trail, the right fork gradually descends to the creek, passing huge, mossy, fern covered boulders and fallen redwoods. To the right are two small campsites surrounded by redwoods. Beyond the camp, the trail is overgrown and hard to follow. Return by retracing your steps.

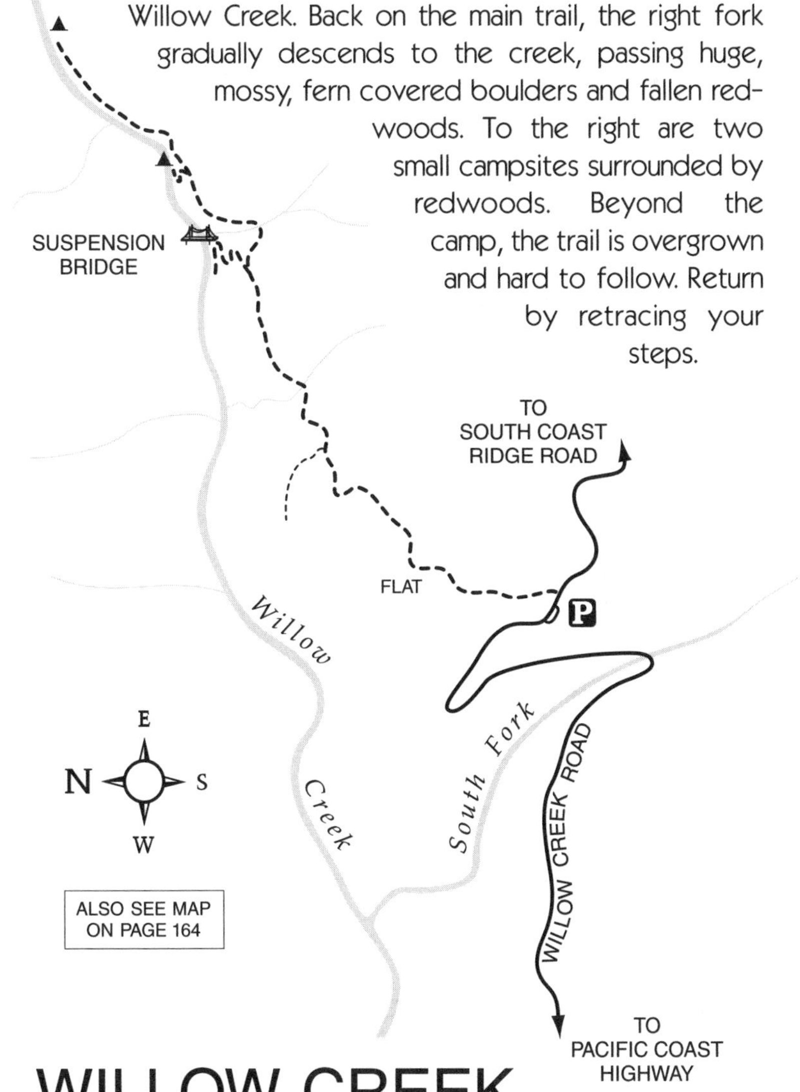

SUSPENSION BRIDGE

TO SOUTH COAST RIDGE ROAD

FLAT

Willow

Creek

South Fork

WILLOW CREEK ROAD

TO PACIFIC COAST HIGHWAY

E

N S

W

ALSO SEE MAP ON PAGE 164

WILLOW CREEK TRAIL

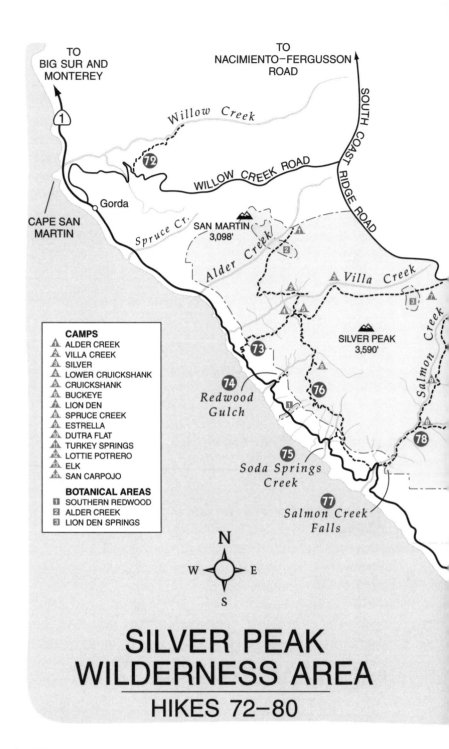

TO
BIG SUR AND
MONTEREY

TO
NACIMIENTO–FERGUSSON
ROAD

SOUTH COAST RIDGE ROAD

Willow Creek

WILLOW CREEK ROAD

Gorda

CAPE SAN
MARTIN

Spruce Cr.

SAN MARTIN
3,098'

Alder Creek

Villa Creek

Salmon Creek

SILVER PEAK
3,590'

Redwood Gulch

Soda Springs Creek

Salmon Creek Falls

CAMPS
△	ALDER CREEK
△	VILLA CREEK
△	SILVER
△	LOWER CRUICKSHANK
△	CRUICKSHANK
△	BUCKEYE
△	LION DEN
△	SPRUCE CREEK
△	ESTRELLA
△	DUTRA FLAT
△	TURKEY SPRINGS
△	LOTTIE POTRERO
△	ELK
△	SAN CARPOJO

BOTANICAL AREAS
1	SOUTHERN REDWOOD
2	ALDER CREEK
3	LION DEN SPRINGS

N
W — E
S

SILVER PEAK
WILDERNESS AREA
HIKES 72–80

Located in the Santa Lucia Range of the Los Padres National Forest is the rugged Silver Peak Wilderness, established in 1992. This remote 14,500-acre wilderness at the southwestern corner of Monterey County is home to California's southern-most coastal redwoods. Three year-round creeks—Villa Creek, Salmon Creek and San Carpoforo Creek—flow from the upper mountain reaches to the sea. A group of steep intersecting trails weave through this wilderness from the ocean to the mountain ridge, gaining nearly 3,600 feet within a couple of miles. The trails wind through open meadows, forest groves, lush stream-fed canyons and ridgelines with sweeping coastal views.

Hike 73
Cruickshank Trail
to Upper Cruickshank Camp

Hiking distance: 5 miles round trip
Hiking time: 3 hours
Elevation gain: 1,200 feet
Maps: U.S.G.S. Villa Creek
           Los Padres National Forest Northern Section Trail Map

Summary of hike: The Cruickshank Trail begins from Highway 1 and climbs the exposed oceanfront hillside to magnificent coastal vistas before dropping into Villa Creek Canyon. The lush canyon path winds through giant redwood groves to Lower and Upper Cruickshank Camps in oak shaded pastureland.

Driving directions: From the Big Sur Ranger Station, located 27 miles south of Carmel, drive 39.6 miles south on Highway 1 to the grassy parking pullout on the east (inland) side of the road by the signed Cruickshank trailhead.

From Highway 1 at Ragged Point, 1.5 miles south of the Monterey County line, drive 7.9 miles north to the trailhead on the right.

Hiking directions: From the signed trailhead, climb switchbacks up the brushy mountain slope. Wind through the thick coastal scrub overlooking the ocean and offshore rocks. More switchbacks lead up the exposed south-facing slope to a ridge with sweeping coastal vistas at 900 feet. Descend a short distance into Villa Creek Canyon above the coastal redwoods carpeting the canyon floor. Traverse the south canyon slope through lush vegetation under oak and redwood groves. Pass the unexplained "Hjalmur's Loop" sign, and continue through the shade of the redwoods. Emerge from the forest to a picturesque view of the ocean, framed by the V-shaped canyon walls. Reenter the forest, passing a tall stand of narrow eucalyptus trees on the left. Cross a log plank over a seasonal stream to Lower Cruickshank Camp fifty yards ahead, a small camp with room for one tent. A quarter mile further is Upper Cruickshank Camp in a large oak flat. This is our turnaround spot.

To extend the hike, two trails depart from the camp. To the left, the north Buckeye Trail crosses a stream by a giant redwood and descends 0.6 miles to Villa Creek Camp in a dense redwood grove at Villa Creek. To the right, the combined Cruickshank and Buckeye Trails cross through the camp to an oak dotted grassland and a posted junction. The Buckeye Trail bears right and heads 3 miles south to Buckeye Camp (Hike 76). To the left, the Cruickshank Trail climbs 500 feet in 1 mile to Silver Camp and 1,500 feet in 3 miles to Lion Den Camp.

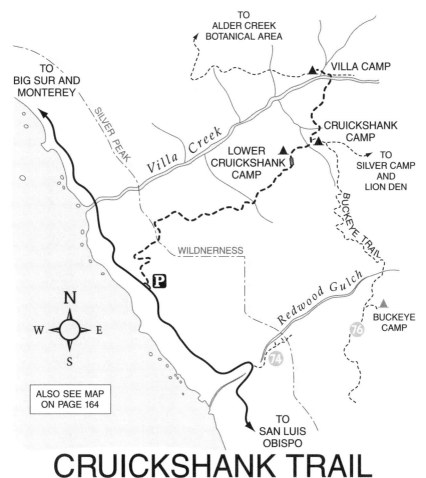

CRUICKSHANK TRAIL

Hike 74
Redwood Gulch
NATHANIEL OWINGS MEMORIAL REDWOOD GROVE

Hiking distance: 0.4 miles round trip
Hiking time: 30 minutes
Elevation gain: 200 feet
Maps: U.S.G.S. Villa Creek
         Los Padres National Forest Northern Section Trail Map

Summary of hike: Redwood Gulch is home to one of California's southernmost groves of coastal redwoods. The gulch is a narrow, eroded gorge with chutes of cascading water, small waterfalls and a myriad of tub-size pools surrounded by huge boulders. This short trail begins at the creek bottom amidst the lush streamside vegetation and climbs through the dank, damp, atmospheric terrain beneath a magnificent stand of imposing redwoods.

Driving directions: From the Big Sur Ranger Station, located 27 miles south of Carmel, drive 40.5 miles south on Highway 1 to the parking pullout on the east (inland) side of the road at the base of the horseshoe shaped bend in the road.

From Highway 1 at Ragged Point, 1.5 miles south of the Monterey County line, drive 7.0 miles north to the trailhead on the right.

Hiking directions: Walk up the wide path along the south side of the creek to the trail sign. Pass a rock fountain and descend to the streambed surrounded by towering redwoods. A short distance ahead is a waterfall, cascading over a jumble of large boulders. At the base of the falls, the water disappears underground. The stream returns above ground west of the highway near the ocean. Continue along the south edge of the waterfall, climbing over fallen redwoods and boulders. Follow the steep path through a wet, dense forest with huge redwoods, boulders and an understory of ferns. Several side paths on the left lead down to pools and smaller waterfalls. At just

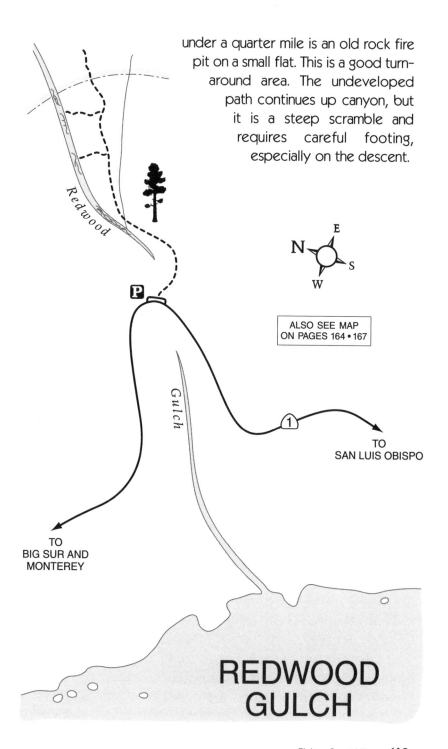

under a quarter mile is an old rock fire pit on a small flat. This is a good turn-around area. The undeveloped path continues up canyon, but it is a steep scramble and requires careful footing, especially on the descent.

Redwood

N
E
S
W

ALSO SEE MAP
ON PAGES 164 • 167

P

Gulch

1

TO
SAN LUIS OBISPO

TO
BIG SUR AND
MONTEREY

REDWOOD
GULCH

Hike 75
Soda Springs and Lower Buckeye Trails

Hiking distance: 3 miles round trip
Hiking time: 1.5 hours
Elevation gain: 750 feet
Maps: U.S.G.S. Burro Mountain
       Los Padres National Forest Northern Section Trail Map

Summary of hike: The Soda Springs Trail begins along Soda Springs Creek in the lush riparian vegetation of ferns, alders and California bay laurel. The trail climbs the forested slope to an overlook with coastal views that extend south to the Point Piedras Blancas lighthouse and Point Buchon, beyond Morro Bay. The path descends to the Salmon Creek drainage, where there are magnificent views of Salmon Creek Falls.

Driving directions: From the Big Sur Ranger Station, located 27 miles south of Carmel, drive 42.2 miles south on Highway 1 to the paved parking pullout on the east (inland) side of the road by the signed Soda Springs trailhead.
    From Highway 1 at Ragged Point, 1.5 miles south of the Monterey County line, drive 5.3 miles north to the trailhead on the right.

Hiking directions: At the trailhead, a left fork drops down to Soda Springs Creek by a waterfall and pool in a rock gorge. The Soda Springs Trail stays to the right and heads up the hill parallel to the creek to an unsigned junction. Bear right, away from the creek, and steadily gain elevation. Thread your way through verdant undergrowth on the shaded forest path. Cross a seasonal stream by a huge boulder, reaching a posted junction with the Buckeye Trail at a coastal overlook. The left fork continues to Buckeye Camp (Hike 76). This hike stays to the right on the lower portion of the Buckeye Trail. Cross through the stock gate, and traverse the hillside parallel to the coastline. The path levels out on a grassy plateau with sweeping oceanfront views. Descend from the ridge on the open slope with a great view of Salmon Creek Falls. Pass a water trough by an underground spring, and cross through two more trail gates. A few short switchbacks quickly descend the hill to the Buckeye Trailhead by the Salmon Creek Ranger Station. This is our turn-around spot. Return along the same route.

To extend the hike to Salmon Creek Falls, follow Highway 1 downhill (left) 0.1 mile to Salmon Creek, and follow the hiking directions for Hike 77.

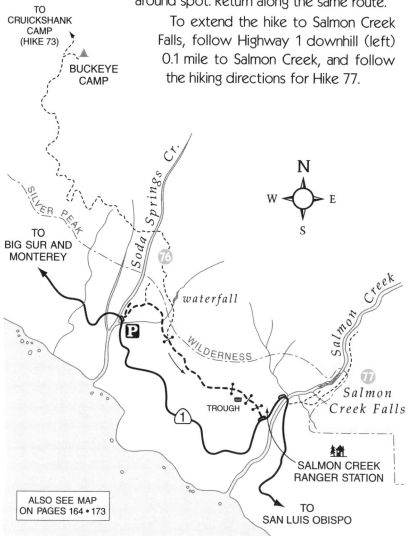

SODA SPRINGS
LOWER BUCKEYE TRAILS

Hike 76
Buckeye Trail to Buckeye Camp

Hiking distance: 7 miles round trip
Hiking time: 4 hours
Elevation gain: 1,600 feet
Maps: U.S.G.S. Burro Mountain and Villa Creek
        Los Padres National Forest Northern Section Trail Map

Summary of hike: Buckeye Camp sits in a large sloping meadow in the mountainous interior of the Silver Peak Wilderness. The camp has a developed spring, picnic bench and rock fire pit under a canopy of an immense bay tree with expansive overhanging branches. The trail begins from the Salmon Creek Ranger Station and climbs the exposed coastal slopes to views of Salmon Creek Falls and the Pacific. The path weaves in and out of several small canyons with shaded oak groves and passes an ephemeral 30-foot waterfall.

Driving directions: From the Big Sur Ranger Station, located 27 miles south of Carmel, drive 43.7 miles south on Highway 1 to the paved parking area on the inland side of the road by the Salmon Creek Ranger Station.

From Highway 1 at Ragged Point, 1.5 miles south of the Monterey County line, drive 3.8 miles north to the trailhead on the right.

Hiking directions: Walk through the trailhead gate at the north end of the parking area. Ascend the hillside on a few short switchbacks, passing through a second trail gate. Climb through the chaparral and grasslands, passing a trough and underground spring to a third gate. The path levels out on a grassy plateau that overlooks Salmon Creek Falls and the ocean. Traverse the hillside high above the ocean, and pass through a gate to a posted Y-fork at 1 mile. The Soda Springs Trail (Hike 75) bears left, returning to Highway 1 at Soda Springs Creek. Take the Buckeye Trail to the right. Cross a stream-fed gully with a seasonal waterfall off a sheer moss covered rock wall. Climb out of the gully, following the contours of the mountains in and out of small oak shaded canyons. Cross Soda Springs Creek at 2 miles to a grassy ridge a half mile ahead, where there are sweeping vistas from the coastline to the ridges and wooded canyons of the Santa Lucia range. Follow the exposed ridge uphill to an elevated perch in an open pine grove above Redwood Gulch. Curve inland and descend into the rolling mountainous interior, reaching Buckeye Camp at 3.5 miles. Return along the same trail. To extend the hike, the Buckeye Trail continues 2.5 miles to Upper Cruickshank Camp (Hike 73).

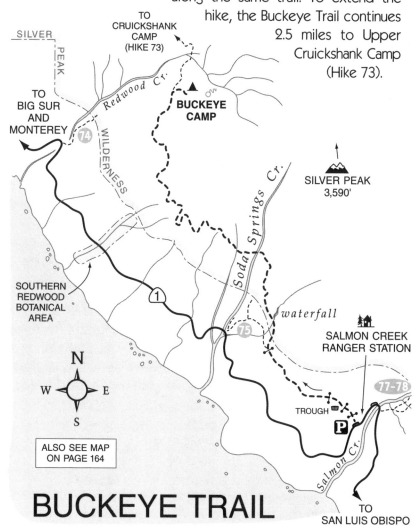

BUCKEYE TRAIL

Hike 77
Salmon Creek Falls
from Salmon Creek Trail

Hiking distance: 0.6 miles round trip
Hiking time: 20 minutes
Elevation gain: 150 feet
Maps: U.S.G.S. Burro Mountain

Summary of hike: The Salmon Creek Trail runs through the deep interior of the Silver Peak Wilderness. This short hike follows the first portion of the trail to the dynamic Salmon Creek Falls, where a tremendous amount of rushing water plunges from three chutes. The water drops more than 100 feet off the Santa Lucia Mountains onto the rocks and pools below. A cool mist sprays over the mossy green streamside vegetation under a shady landscape of alders and laurels.

Driving directions: From the Big Sur Ranger Station, located 27 miles south of Carmel, drive 43.8 miles south on Highway 1 to the signed Salmon Creek trailhead and wide pullout on the left.

From Highway 1 at Ragged Point, 1.5 miles south of the Monterey County line, drive 3.7 miles north to the trailhead on the right.

Hiking directions: Walk alongside the guardrail to the signed trailhead on the south side of Salmon Creek. Salmon Creek Falls can be seen from the guardrail. Take the Salmon Creek Trail up the gorge into the lush, verdant forest. Pass an old wooden gate, and cross a small tributary stream. Two hundred yards ahead is a signed junction. The right fork continues on the Salmon Creek Trail (Hike 78). Take the left fork towards the falls. Cross another small stream, then descend around huge boulders towards Salmon Creek at the base of the falls. Head towards the thunderous sound of the waterfall. Climb around the wet boulders to explore the various caves and overlooks.

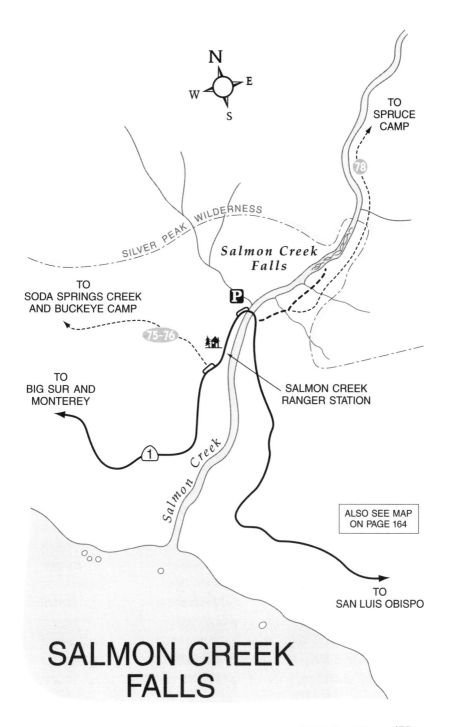

N
W E
S

TO
SPRUCE
CAMP

78

SILVER PEAK WILDERNESS

Salmon Creek Falls

TO
SODA SPRINGS CREEK
AND BUCKEYE CAMP

P

75-76

TO
BIG SUR AND
MONTEREY

SALMON CREEK
RANGER STATION

1

Salmon Creek

ALSO SEE MAP
ON PAGE 164

TO
SAN LUIS OBISPO

SALMON CREEK
FALLS

Hike 78
Salmon Creek Trail
to Spruce and Estrella Camps

Hiking distance: 6.5 miles round trip
Hiking time: 3.5 hours
Elevation gain: 1,300 feet
Maps: U.S.G.S. Burro Mountain
Los Padres National Forest Northern Section Trail Map

Summary of hike: The Salmon Creek Trail begins by Salmon Creek Falls (Hike 77) and follows the southeast wall of the canyon through forests and open slopes. There are far reaching views up the canyon and down to the ocean. The trail, which cuts across the Silver Peak Wilderness, leads to Spruce Camp and Estrella Camp. Estrella Camp sits in a large grassy meadow under the shade of oak, pine and madrone trees. After crossing Spruce Creek, the cliffside path parallels Salmon Creek, overlooking endless cascades, small waterfalls and pools.

Driving directions: Same as Hike 77.

Hiking directions: Head up the forested canyon on the south side of Salmon Creek to a junction at 200 yards. The left fork drops down a short distance to Salmon Creek Falls—Hike 77. Take the right fork, heading up the hillside to an overlook of Highway 1 and the Pacific. The path winds through the fir forest, steadily gaining elevation to a clearing high above Salmon Creek. The sweeping vistas extend up Salmon Creek canyon and down across the ocean. Follow the contours of the south canyon wall, with small dips and rises, to a posted junction with the Spruce Creek Trail at 1.9 miles. Stay to the left and descend a quarter mile to Spruce Camp on the banks of Spruce Creek. Cross Spruce Creek on a log bridge just above Salmon Creek. Follow Salmon Creek upstream on the southeast canyon slope, overlooking a long series of cascades, pools and waterfalls. Continually ascend the contour above the creek, crossing an old mudslide. The trail levels out on a grassy flat and enters the shady Estrella Camp at 1,500 feet. Descend 50 yards to the Estrella Fork of Salmon Creek, just beyond the camp. This is our turnaround area.

The trail continues past the creek, climbing 1,800 feet in 2.5 miles to the South Coast Ridge Road.

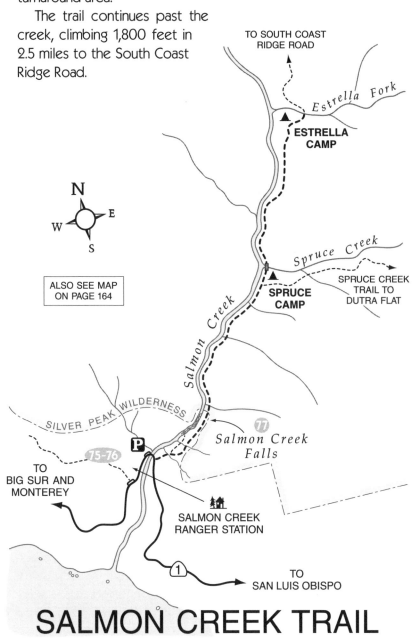

TO SOUTH COAST
RIDGE ROAD

Estrella Fork

▲
**ESTRELLA
CAMP**

N
E
W
S

Spruce Creek

ALSO SEE MAP
ON PAGE 164

▲
**SPRUCE
CAMP**

SPRUCE CREEK
TRAIL TO
DUTRA FLAT

Salmon Creek

WILDERNESS

SILVER PEAK

77

*Salmon Creek
Falls*

P

75-76

TO
BIG SUR AND
MONTEREY

SALMON CREEK
RANGER STATION

1

TO
SAN LUIS OBISPO

SALMON CREEK TRAIL

Hike 79
Nature and Cliffside Trails
Ragged Point Inn

Hiking distance: 1 mile round trip
Hiking time: 30 minutes
Elevation gain: 300 feet
Maps: U.S.G.S. Burro Mountain

Summary of hike: The Ragged Point Cliffside Trail cuts across the edge of a steep, rugged, north-facing cliff where the San Luis Obispo coast turns into the Big Sur coast. The trail ends at the black sand beach and rocky shore at the base of Black Swift Falls, a 300-foot tiered waterfall. Benches are perched on the cliff for great views of the sheer coastal mountains plunging into the sea. The Ragged Point Nature Trail follows the perimeter of the peninsula along the high blufftop terrace. There are several scenic vista points and an overlook.

Driving directions: From Cambria, drive 23 miles north on Highway 1 to the Ragged Point Inn and Restaurant on the left. Turn left and park in the paved lot.

From the Monterey County line, drive 1.5 miles south on Highway 1 to the Ragged Point Inn and Restaurant on the right.

Hiking directions: Take the gravel path west (between the snack bar and gift shop) towards the point. Fifty yards ahead is a signed junction at a grassy overlook. The Nature Trail continues straight ahead, circling the blufftop terrace through windswept pine and cypress trees. At the northwest point is a viewing platform. Waterfalls can be seen cascading off the cliffs on both sides of the promontory. Back at the junction, the Cliffside Trail descends down the steps over the cliff's edge past a bench and across a wooden bridge. Switchbacks cut across the edge of the steep cliff to the base of Black Swift Falls at the sandy beach. After enjoying the surroundings, head back up the steep path.

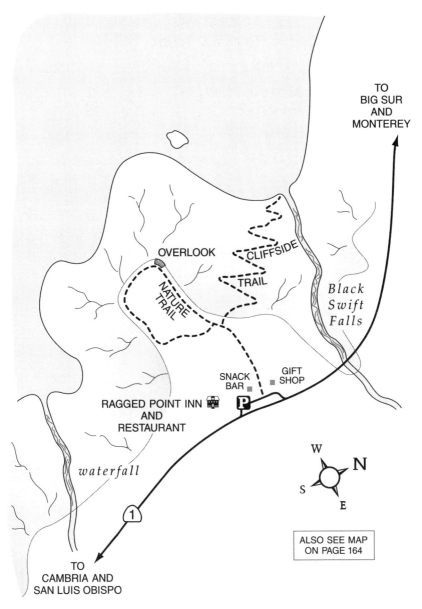

TO
BIG SUR
AND
MONTEREY

OVERLOOK

CLIFFSIDE

TRAIL

NATURE
TRAIL

*Black
Swift
Falls*

SNACK
BAR

GIFT
SHOP

RAGGED POINT INN
AND
RESTAURANT

P

waterfall

W N

S

E

1

TO
CAMBRIA AND
SAN LUIS OBISPO

ALSO SEE MAP
ON PAGE 164

NATURE and CLIFFSIDE TRAILS
RAGGED POINT INN

Hike 80
Ragged Point

Hiking distance: 0.8 miles round trip
Hiking time: 30 minutes
Elevation gain: 40 feet
Maps: U.S.G.S. Burro Mountain

Summary of hike: This hike crosses a marine terrace to Ragged Point, which is actually located 1.8 miles south of the Ragged Point Inn (Hike 79). From the point are overlooks of the scalloped coastline, a sandy beach cove, offshore rocks pounded by the surf, and Bald Top rising from the Santa Lucia Mountains. San Carpoforo Creek empties into the ocean north of Ragged Point. The well-defined trail crosses through Hearst Corporation ranchland to the headland. Although there are no public easements, the well-defined trails have been used by surfers, fishermen and hikers for many years. Portions of the bluff top cliffs are unstable and caution is advised.

Driving directions: From Cambria, drive 21 miles north on Highway 1 to a large, unsigned dirt turnoff on the left, on a right bend in the road. Turning left here is dangerous. Instead, continue 0.4 miles past the turnoff, and turn around after crossing the bridge over San Carpoforo Creek.

From the Ragged Point Inn and Restaurant, located 1.5 miles south of the Monterey County line, drive 1.8 miles south on Highway 1 to the wide turnout on the right, 0.4 miles south of the San Carpoforo Creek bridge.

Hiking directions: Cross over the fence and follow the wide path west. Walk through a scrub brush meadow backed by the towering Santa Lucia Mountains. Enter a shady canopy of twisted pines on the soft pine needle path. Emerge from the forest to the edge of the 100-foot bluffs. From the north-facing cliffs of Ragged Point are views below of a crescent-shaped beach with magnificent rock outcroppings. Several paths weave along the bluffs to additional coastal views. A narrow, razor-edged path leads west to the point. If you choose to venture west, exercise caution and good judgement.

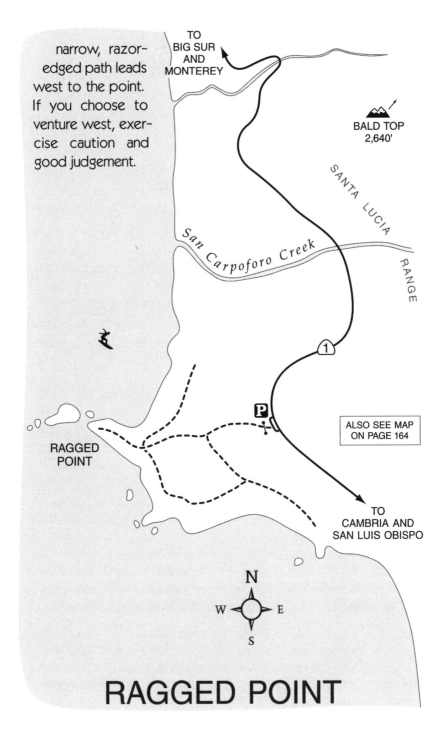

TO
BIG SUR
AND
MONTEREY

BALD TOP
2,640'

SANTA LUCIA RANGE

San Carpoforo Creek

1

P

ALSO SEE MAP
ON PAGE 164

RAGGED
POINT

TO
CAMBRIA AND
SAN LUIS OBISPO

N
W E
S

RAGGED POINT

DAY HIKE
BOOKS

DAY HIKES ON THE
California
Central
Coast
71 GREAT HIKES
Robert Stone

DAY HIKES ON THE
California
Southern
Coast
100 GREAT HIKES
Robert Stone

DAY HIKES AROUND
Monterey
& Carmel
77 GREAT HIKES
Robert Stone

DAY HIKES AROUND
Big Sur
80 GREAT HIKES
Robert Stone

DAY HIKES IN
SAN LUIS OBISPO
COUNTY
CALIFORNIA
ROBERT STONE

DAY HIKES AROUND
Santa
Barbara
82 GREAT HIKES
Robert Stone
2nd EDITION

DAY HIKES AROUND
Ventura
County
82 GREAT HIKES
Robert Stone
2nd EDITION

LOS ANGELES TIMES BESTSELLER
DAY HIKES AROUND
Los
Angeles
82 GREAT HIKES
Robert Stone
4th EDITION

DAY HIKES AROUND
Orange
County
108 GREAT HIKES
Robert Stone

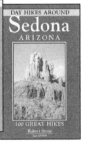
DAY HIKES AROUND
Sedona
ARIZONA
100 GREAT HIKES
Robert Stone
2nd EDITION

DAY HIKES IN
Yosemite
NATIONAL PARK
55 GREAT HIKES
Robert Stone
2nd EDITION

DAY HIKES IN
Sequoia
&
Kings Canyon
NATIONAL PARKS
Robert Stone

DAY HIKES ON
Oahu
57 GREAT HIKES
Robert Stone
2nd EDITION

DAY HIKES ON
Maui
55 GREAT HIKES
Robert Stone
3rd EDITION

DAY HIKES ON
Kauai
55 GREAT HIKES
Robert Stone
2nd EDITION

DAY HIKES IN
Yellowstone
NATIONAL PARK
82 GREAT HIKES
Robert Stone
4th EDITION

DAY HIKES IN
Grand
Teton
NATIONAL PARK
72 GREAT HIKES
Robert Stone
4th EDITION

DAY HIKES IN THE
BEARTOOTH
MOUNTAINS
RED LODGE, MONTANA TO
YELLOWSTONE NATIONAL PARK
ROBERT STONE

DAY HIKES AROUND
BOZEMAN
MONTANA
INCLUDING THE GALLATIN
CANYON AND PARADISE VALLEY
ROBERT STONE

DAY HIKES AROUND
Missoula
MONTANA
INCLUDING THE BITTERROOT
AND THE SEELEY-SWAN VALLEY
Robert Stone
2nd EDITION

Notes

About the Author

For more than a decade, veteran hiker Robert Stone has been writer, photographer, and publisher of Day Hike Books. Robert has hiked every trail in the *Day Hike Book* series. With 21 hiking guides in the series, many in their second, third, and fourth editions, he has hiked thousands of miles of trails throughout the western United States and Hawaii. When Robert is not hiking, he researches, writes, and maps the hikes before returning to the trails. He is an active member of OWAC (Outdoor Writers Associaton of California). Robert spends summers in the Rocky Mountains of Montana and winters on the California Central Coast.